Christopher Wordsworth

On the Inspiration of the Bible

Five Lectures

Christopher Wordsworth

On the Inspiration of the Bible
Five Lectures

ISBN/EAN: 9783337183776

Printed in Europe, USA, Canada, Australia, Japan

Cover: Foto ©ninafisch / pixelio.de

More available books at **www.hansebooks.com**

ON

THE INSPIRATION

OF THE

BIBLE:

FIVE LECTURES,

DELIVERED IN WESTMINSTER ABBEY.

BY

CHR. WORDSWORTH D.D.

BISHOP OF LINCOLN.

EIGHTH EDITION.

RIVINGTONS,

London, Oxford, and Cambridge.

1875.

PREFATORY NOTE TO THE EIGHTH EDITION.

THE following Lectures were delivered in Westminster Abbey by the Author when Canon of that church. Attacks on the Veracity and Inspiration of Holy Scripture, which then startled and shocked the Church, have now become more violent and frequent; but they have strengthened the faith of the devout student of Scripture, because they are fulfilments of prophecies which he reads in its pages; and they make him resort with more thankfulness and love to the testimony of Jesus Christ, the Incarnate WORD, who has set His seal on the Written Word.

More than fourteen hundred years ago, St Augustine[1] (when contending against the errors

[1] *S. Augustin.* de Civ. Dei, lib. xi. c. 1. 3. "Ipsa Veritas, DEUS, DEI FILIUS, Mediator Dei et hominum, Homo CHRISTUS JESUS, priùs per Prophetas, deinde per SE IPSUM, posteà per Apostolos, quantum satis esse judicavit, locutus, etiam SCRIPTURAM condidit, quæ CANONICA appellatur, eminentissimæ auctoritatis, cui fidem habemus de iis rebus, quas ignorare non expedit, nec per nosmetipsos nosse idonei sumus."
S. Augustin. c. Faustum ii. c. 5. "Distincta est a posteri-

of the Manichæans concerning Scripture, which have been revived in the nineteenth century, declared a fundamental truth, which ought to be ever present to the mind of the Christian reader. He affirmed that Christ, the Eternal WORD of God is the Giver of the Written Word, and that when for our sakes He became Man, He set His seal upon the Old Testament: and that after His Ascension He enabled the Apostles and Evangelists, by the inspiration of the Holy Ghost,—whom He sent to them from Heaven,—to write the New Testament; and that He is ever present with His Church Universal, and has sent the Holy Ghost to abide with her for ever; and that therefore the witness of the Church Universal to the Genuineness, Veracity and Inspiration of Holy Scripture is no other than the testimony of Christ, the Son of God, and of God the Holy Ghost, the Spirit of Life and Light.

The Ancient Christian Church represented this

oribus libris excellentia CANONICÆ auctoritatis VETERIS et NOVI TESTAMENTI, quæ Apostolorum confirmata temporibus, per successiones Episcopales et propagationes Ecclesiarum tanquam in sede quâdam sublimiter constituta est, cui serviat omnis fidelis et pius Intellectus."

S. Augustine de Consens. Evangel. lib. i. cap. ult. also well says, "Christus, Qui Prophetas *ante* Suam descensionem misit, Ipse et Apostolos *post* Suam ascensionem misit . . . quicquid Ille de Suis factis et dictis nos legere voluit, hoc scribendum illis tanquam Suis manibus imperavit."

great truth by works of Sacred Art. In the Catacombs of Rome she displayed it in frescos[2] pourtraying Christ, seated on a throne, with an Opened Book in His hand—the Bible—its pages turned outward to the spectator. On His right side and on the left, are two *capsæ* or *scrinia*, or cylindrical caskets, containing rolls of papyri,— the Volumes of the Old and New Testament. Further beyond, on the right and left, are two standing figures, representing the two Apostles, St. Peter and St. Paul—the Apostles of the Hebrew and Gentile Churches. By such pictures as these she set forth the doctrine that it is Christ Himself Who speaks in the Bible; and that He also delivers the Bible by means of the ministry of the Apostolic Church Universal to the World.

It has been the design of the Author to develope these truths in the following Lectures.

Riseholme, Epiphany, 1875.

---

[2] Such a fresco may be seen engraved and described in Dideon's "Iconographie Chrétienne," p. 29, Paris 1843, who says, "Ce monument date des premiers siècles de l' Église;" and in the Rev. Wharton Marriott's "Vestiarium Christianum," Plate xii. and p. 235, London, 1868.

CONTENTS.

LECTURE I.

	PAGE
Importance of the subject proposed	1
Attacks upon the Bible in ancient times	2
Prospects for the future	3
The last days will be days of unbelief	ib.
Predictions in the Apocalypse	ib.
Change of opinion in some quarters in England	4
What we mean by *Inspiration*	5
What it is *not*	ib.
Compared to the Transfiguration	ib.
Analogies between the *Written* Word and the *Incarnate* WORD	6
Inspiration and the Incarnation	7
The Writers of Scripture are channels of Divine Truth	7, 8
The HOLY GHOST is the AUTHOR of Prophecy, which came *through* the Prophets	8
There are no Errors in the *genuine, original,* text of the Word of God	9, 10
Destructive consequences of the opposite statement; the objection of a modern Sceptic to some recent theological writers	11
The Bible is for peasants and children; are they to *reject some parts* of it, and *accept others?*	12
Some of the most mysterious parts of the Bible were written by the instrumentality of illiterate men; would this have been the case, if the writers were not to be preserved from error by its Divine Author?	13

	PAGE
As *men*, the Writers of Scripture were fallible in *practice*.	14
But as *writers* of *books*, which have been received as *Holy Scripture* by the Universal Church, which is the mystical Body of Christ, they have *not erred* in *writing*.	15
Why they sometimes speak *doubtingly*	16
The language of Scripture is human, but is under Divine guidance	17, 18
The *Various Readings* in the different Manuscripts of the Hebrew and Greek Originals of the Old and New Testaments, are no evidence of uncertainty; but, on the contrary, are the ground of confidence in the Text of the Bible, which has been formed by the *collations* of different Manuscripts	20
What is the *true* ground of belief in the Inspiration of the Bible?	20
Is our *private consciousness* a sufficient ground?	20, 21
No; *that* is *no* argument to *others;* and *not* a *safe* one to *ourselves*	21, 22
Different persons have different perceptions; and *if* private consciousness were to be admitted as a ground for belief in the inspiration of a Book, we should have a great variety of different and contradictory Books, each admitted to be inspired	23
Calamitous results of this theory in foreign countries	23, 24
It has now been developed in an infidel direction in England	25, 26
Present religious crisis in England	28

LECTURE II.

Recapitulation	30
Private consciousness is not sufficient to prove the Inspiration of the Bible	31
Nor can Scripture itself alone prove its own Inspiration	ib.
What are the true grounds of belief in the Truth and Inspiration of the Old Testament?	32
1. Testimony of GOD, in the reception of the Old Testament by the Jewish Church.	

Contents.

	PAGE
2. Testimony of JESUS CHRIST, the SON of GOD, receiving the Old Testament.	
3. Testimony of God the HOLY GHOST, in the Christian Church—receiving the Old Testament	33
These propositions are now to be proved	ib.
First then, it is to be shown that the Old Testament, which is in *our* hands, is the *same* as the Old Testament in the age of Christ	34
Proof of this	34, 35
How did the Jews of our Lord's age regard the Old Testament?	35, 36
As true and divine	36
Testimony of Josephus to this statement	36, 37
How were they persuaded, that the Old Testament as it was in their age, was *genuine, authentic, true,* and *divine?*	38
Answer to this question; from *external* evidence	39
And from *internal*	40
Original of the Pentateuch enshrined in the Holy of Holies	44
To be copied out by the Kings	45
Inspiration of the Prophetical Books, how proved	47, 48
God's wonderful providence in making the Jews the guardians of the Old Testament	ib.
Completion of the Canon of the Old Testament	49, 50
The external evidences of its truth and inspiration are confirmed by *internal* proofs	51
Reply to a sceptical objection, grounded on the rejection of Christ by the Jews	51, 52
Argument in favour of the truth and inspiration of the Old Testament, from the blindness and unbelief of the Jews	52
Recapitulation of the argument	52, 53
The Testimony of GOD bearing witness in the Hebrew Church to the Truth and Inspiration of the Old Testament is further confirmed by the witness of the SON of GOD, and of GOD the HOLY GHOST in the Christian Church; and thus the belief in the truth and inspiration of the Old Testament rests on the authority of the THREE PERSONS of the BLESSED TRINITY—	
This proposition to be proved in the next Lectures	54

LECTURE III.

	PAGE
On the Testimony of JESUS CHRIST to the Old Testament	56
First, it is to be shown that the four Gospels are *true*	ib.
Proof of their truth	57—60
Inferences from this proof: CHRIST is GOD, and knows all things, and came to bear witness to the Truth	61
How did *He* treat the Old Testament?	63
He *agreed* with the Jews, who received the *whole* of it as *true*, and as *inspired*	63, 64
Evidence of this	64, 65
Christ's testimony to the Old Testament at the Temptation —and in the Synagogues,—in His public teaching; and after His Resurrection	64—66
Allegations considered, (1) that Jesus Christ spoke only "as a learned Jewish Rabbi;" and (2) that He "*accommodated* Himself to the popular opinions of the Jews"	67, 68
Testimony of GOD the HOLY GHOST to the truth and inspiration of the Old Testament	69
Appeal to the authority of Christ in reply to sceptical objections against portions of the Old Testament; e.g. From Geology and other physical sciences; and from Moral or Metaphysical speculations	69—72
Moral *use* of *difficulties* in the Old Testament; such as the standing still of the Sun at the bidding of Joshua; the histories of Balaam, and Jonah, &c. Book of Daniel	73—76
We enjoy far greater advantages with regard to the Old Testament than were possessed by the *Jews;* and our responsibilities are proportional to our privileges	77
Holy Scripture is set for our moral probation; and our eternal happiness depends on our use of it	78, 80

LECTURE IV.

What are the grounds of our belief in the Inspiration of the *New* Testament?	81
It has been proved that the Gospels are *true*	83

	PAGE
In those Gospels (proved to be true) we have certain declarations from Christ (Who in those Gospels is shown to be GOD) concerning the Church, which He has founded	84
He promised to send the HOLY GHOST to *teach her all things;* to *guide* her into *all truth,* and to *abide* with her for ever	ib.
The Apostles and Evangelists, being taught by the HOLY GHOST, wrote the *New* Testament; which has been received, as true and as divinely inspired, by the HOLY GHOST dwelling in the Universal Church, which is the body *of Christ,* the *Pillar and Ground of Truth;* and is publicly read by her as of *equal* authority with the *Old* Testament which Jesus Christ, the SON of GOD, received as *true* and *inspired*	84–86
Analogy in the means used by God for preserving and authenticating *both* Testaments	86
Purposes served by the public reading of the New Testament in the Church	88
Why some smaller portions of the New Testament were not received at once	90
The Church does not *give* authority to Scripture: but bears witness that Scripture is *given* by inspiration of God	92
Review of the reasons for which we receive Scripture, on the testimony of the Church	92, 93
The wisdom of the Church of England in regard to this question of Inspiration	93
Her principles contrasted with those of some other religious bodies	93, 94
The Church Universal is the Candlestick in which the Light of Scripture is placed by God	95
They who separate the Light from the Candlestick are in danger of losing both	98
Moral requisites for receiving the Bible as true and inspired	99
The *internal* evidence of the truth and inspiration of the Bible confirms the *external*	101
Anticipations of a future State when HOLY SCRIPTURE will be more fully understood	102

LECTURE V.

	PAGE
Recapitulation of the argument in behalf of the truth and inspiration of the Bible	103
That argument is confirmed by the evidence of God's providential care of the Bible	106—109
Illustrated by reference to the history of the Bible in England	110
The fulfilment of the Prophecies of the Bible also confirms the proof of its truth and inspiration . - .	112
That proof is still further confirmed by the harmony of the several parts of the Bible	113
The weakness of the instruments used in writing the Bible, and the effects produced by their instrumentality, is a further confirmation of the truth that the Bible is from God	114
The beneficial changes wrought in the world by the Bible are also evidences of its divine origin . .	115—118
Testimony of the English Nation to the divine origin of the Bible	119
Meditations on the truth and inspiration of the Bible, suggested by the Abbey Church of Westminster .	120—122
Proofs of the divine power of the HOLY BIBLE at death-beds, and in the prospect of Eternity . . .	123
The Day of Judgment will prove the truth of the Bible .	ib.
Conclusion	ib.

LECTURE I.

---

1 PETER iii. 15.

Be ready always to give an answer to every man that asketh you a reason of the hope that is in you.

I. 1. THE hope that is in us as Christians rests upon the belief that the Bible is the Word of God. The works of the natural Creation declare His Power, but they do not reveal to us the Mysteries of Faith. Human Reason could never have assured us that sinners may obtain pardon through God's mercy in a Redeemer, and that we may also obtain spiritual grace, enabling us to do His Will. We could never have discovered by our intellectual faculties, that there is a Judgment to come, and a Resurrection of the Body, and joys eternal in heaven for those who believe and obey Him.

These are supernatural truths, and they are revealed to us in the Bible, and in the Bible alone. And by faith in these truths we are excited to do our duty to God, our neighbour, and ourselves: we are encouraged to suffer patiently, and *to live soberly, righteously, and godly in this present world, looking for that blessed hope, and the glorious appearing of the great God and our Saviour Jesus Christ*[1]. Therefore the Apostle St. Paul says, *Whatsoever things were written aforetime were written for our learning, that we through patience and comfort of the Scriptures might have hope*[2].

2. Our spiritual Enemy knows, that belief in the INSPIRATION of the BIBLE is the foundation of all Christian faith and Christian virtue; and that, if "the belief in the authority of Scripture is shaken, then Christian faith will falter, and if Christian faith falters, then Christian love will fail[3]," and that the fabric of human Society will be dissolved, and that men and nations will become victims of his power, and be involved in confusion and ruin.

The Evil One has therefore been indefatigable in his attempts to shake this foundation. In ancient days he enlisted Kings against the Bible. He incited Antiochus Epiphanes to take up arms against the Old Testament. He raised up the Emperor Diocletian against the New. He engaged sceptical philosophers, such as Celsus, Porphyry, and Julian, in an intellectual campaign against the Word of God. He beguiled some, who called themselves Christians, to impugn the Bible. The

---

[1] Titus ii. 12, 13. [2] Rom. xv. 4.
[3] *S. Augustine* de Doct. Christianâ i. 41, "Titubabit fides, si divinarum Scripturarum vacillat auctoritas; porrò, fide titubante, charitas et etiam ipsa languescet." And so *Hooker* (III. viii. 13) says, "The main principle whereupon our belief of all things therein contained dependeth, is that the Scriptures are the Oracles of God."

Marcionites and the Manichæans alleged that the Old Testament is contrary to the New. Other heretical Teachers rejected portions of both Testaments, others distorted their meaning by novel interpretations, and substituted their own imaginations in the place of the Word of God.

The Church of God, with the Bible in her hands, regards the past with thankfulness, and looks forward to the future with hope. She knows that the Holy Scriptures have already passed through a severe ordeal; and she is sure, that their Divine Author, Who has never failed to protect them, will defend them unto the end. She is persuaded that all attacks upon the Bible will issue in its victory, and will manifest more clearly that it is the Word of God.

As the end of the world draws near, the Bible may expect new conflicts, and may hope for new conquests. The Bible will be treated as Christ was treated by the World. The career of the Written Word will be like that of the INCARNATE WORD. *It* will have *its* Gethsemane, and its Calvary; but it will have also its glorious Resurrection and Ascension. Its prophecies concerning itself will be fulfilled. *The Two Witnesses* will *preach in sackcloth* [4]. That is, the Two Testaments will preach in sorrow. They may seem to be dead; but they will revive and be caught up into heaven, and all their foes will be confounded. The Enemy

---

[4] See Rev. xi. 3, 4. The author begs leave to refer to the exposition of that prophecy in his notes on the passage.

of Holy Scripture will rage more fiercely, in proportion as his doom is nearer. He will make more desperate assaults upon Holy Writ, knowing that *he hath but a short time*[5]. But it will triumph, and be glorified, and judge the world. (John xii. 48.)

3. England has hitherto stood high among the Nations of the World, during some centuries, for her reverent esteem of the Bible. But now a change seems to be taking place. Persons eminent for high position in our Schools of Learning and in the Church, and exercising great influence, have not hesitated to avow an opinion, that portions of Holy Scripture are blemished by error, and cannot have come from Him who is the Truth.

Such affirmations as these require us to examine the grounds of our own belief in the Inspiration of Holy Writ. And since it is our duty to promote the temporal and eternal happiness of others, as well as our own, we ought to be prepared to give an *answer to every one who asks us a reason of the hope that is in us.*

This then is the question before us—

By what reasons are we persuaded, and by what arguments would we persuade others, that the Bible is the Word of God?

II. In dealing with this subject, let us first explain what we mean when we say that the Scriptures are *inspired* by God.

[5] Rev. xii. 12.

1. We do *not* intend thereby to affirm, that the Writers of Holy Scripture were *constrained* to write, without any volition or consciousness on their part. David, singing the Psalms, was not like the Harp in David's hand. It was a mechanical instrument, but he was a free agent. The Holy Ghost inspired the writers of Holy Scripture. *Holy men*, says St. Peter[6], *spake, being moved or borne along*[7] *by the Holy Ghost. All Scripture is given by inspiration of God*, says St. Paul[8]. It is animated by His Divine breath[9]. But He did not impair their moral and intellectual faculties, nor destroy their personal identity.

Inspiration may be called a spiritual *Transfiguration*. At the Transfiguration of Christ on the Holy Mount, as described in the Gospels, Moses and Elias *appeared in glory*[10]. Moses the Giver of the Law was there, and Elias the greatest of the Prophets. They were *transfigured*. But Moses *retained his identity;* so did Elias. Moses was still Moses, and Elias was still Elias. Each was recognized by the Disciples, Peter, James, and John.

So it is with the Writers of Holy Scripture.

[6] 2 Pet. i. 21.

[7] φερόμενοι, *carried along* like a ship by the wind, or like a vessel on a stream. In this text the Vatican Manuscript has ἐλάλησαν ἀπὸ Θεοῦ ἄνθρωποι, i. e. *men spake from God;* and this reading gives greater force to the assertion of their Divine Inspiration.

[8] 2 Tim. iii. 16.   [9] θεόπνευστος.

[10] Matt. xvii. 2, 3.   Luke ix. 30, 31,   Cf. 2 Pet. i. 18.

Moses, when inspired, was raised above Moses uninspired. St. Peter, St. John, and St. Paul, when writing Holy Scripture, were lifted above themselves by the power of the Holy Ghost. They were raised above their own level, and that of this lower world, and were placed as it were on a "holy mount." In Scripture, the Holy men, through whose instrumentality we have received the Law, the Prophecies, and the Gospels, are joined together with Christ, as it were, on a Mountain of Transfiguration; they are illumined by His glorious light, and the cloud of His presence overshadows them. But each of them *retains* his *identity*, each shines in his own sphere: they are spiritualized and glorified; they are *transfigured*.

In the *written* Word of God there is a holy union of human with divine, and we are not able to draw the line, where what is human ends, and what is divine begins. This union of human with divine in the *Written Word*, bears some resemblance to one of the greatest Mysteries of our faith, the union of God with Man in the INCARNATE WORD. The Inspiration of Scripture may be compared to the Incarnation of Christ. Jesus Christ is *Emmanuel, God with us*[1], *God manifest in the flesh*[2]. The two Natures of God and Man are joined together in His One Person. But who can draw the line, where God's nature ends, and where Man's nature begins, in the Person of Christ? The union of God and Man in the *Incarnate Word*

---

[1] Matt. i. 23.   [2] 1 Tim. iii. 16.

is a Mystery. So is the union of the Divine element with the human in the *Written Word*. In both cases the Mystery baffles our powers of analysis. In both cases the Mystery, like the mid-day sun in the heavens, dazzles the eye with its brightness; we cannot gaze upon it. But, in both cases also, the Mystery, like the Sun in the heavens, *enables us to see*. All would be dim in the spiritual world, without the light of the Incarnate Word, and of the Written Word. And in both cases it is the union of Divinity with Humanity, which is the cause of spiritual light.

Let us illustrate this by another comparison. Holy Scripture is *God's Word written*. The things written are *from* God; *all Scripture is given by Inspiration of God*. The fresh and living Water of heavenly Truth issues from one Source, and that Source is Divine; but the water flows in various streams. The Fountain is Divine, the element is heavenly; but the channels are earthly, and the channels do not change the essential quality of the water, but they modify its direction and its course, and tinge it, as it were, with the colour of the soil of the banks through which the water flows. The heavenly water acts upon the earthly margins of the streams; and the margins act upon the water; they act and react upon each other with a simultaneous and concurrent operation. Sometimes the Divine element of Inspired Truth rushes vehemently in torrents and in cataracts, in the impetuous fervour of St.

Paul. Sometimes it diffuses itself, and sleeps in calm and deep lakes, in the love and gentleness of St. John. The Element is one and the same, and Divine; the channels are different, and human; the power of the one destroys not the liberty of the other; Divine Grace does not annul the human intellect and will, though it is suggestive, preventive, suppletory, auxiliary to them; but the Divine Spirit, and the human Intellect and Will, concur and act together in loving harmony and joy.

2. In accordance with this statement it may be remarked, that the prophecies of the Old Testament are described in Scripture as coming to us *through* (διὰ) the Prophets. This is the manner in which the prophecies of the Old Testament are quoted in the New[3]. The Holy Ghost is the *Author* of the prophecies which are delivered by the Prophets. He is the Everlasting Fountain; the Prophecy is the living water, the Prophet is the *channel, through* which it flows.

3. We affirm, then, that there is a human element in Holy Scripture; but we assert also that this human element is refined, sublimed, spiritualized, and purified from the taint of human error, in the Word of God. We are not among those who say, that Holy Scripture is marred and blemished by imperfections and inaccuracies. We cannot concur with some who affirm that there are historical inaccuracies in the Pentateuch

---

[3] Matt. ii. 5. 15. 17. 23; iii. 3; iv. 14, &c.

and in the Books of Joshua and the Judges, and of Samuel. We cannot agree in the assertion that the Holy Evangelist St. Matthew errs in his exposition of the Prophecies recited in his first and second chapters. We cannot allow that St. Matthew and St. Luke are at variance with one another in their narratives of the incidents of our Lord's infancy; we cannot concede that St. Mark errs when he says that David ate the shewbread in the days of Abiathar the High Priest[4]. We cannot admit, that St. Luke errs, in saying that the Taxing at the Nativity took place in the time of Cyrenius[5]. We cannot grant, that St. John errs, when he says that the Chief Priests had not eaten the Passover on the day of the Crucifixion[6]. We cannot concede that either he[7] or St. Mark[8] errs in their record of the hour on which the Crucifixion took place. We know that these allegations may be, and have been refuted; and we deliberately state our conviction, that while there are sundry *varieties* serving to complete the Evangelical history, there is *no contradiction* in it[9].

Again; we cannot concur with those who say that there are historical mistakes in St. Stephen's speech to the Hebrew Sanhedrim[1], and that there-

---

[4] Mark ii. 26. [5] Luke ii. 2. [6] John xviii. 18.
[7] John xix. 14. [8] Mark xv. 25.
[9] Cp. *Euseb.* Demonst. Evang. iii. 5, and *S. Augustine's* treatise De Consensu Evangelistarum, and the notes on these passages in my edition of the Greek Testament.
[1] See on Acts vii. Cp. the case of Deborah speaking of Jael: and my notes at end of Judges iv.

fore the Author of the Acts of the Apostles errs when he says that St. Stephen was *full of the Holy Ghost*, and that *no one could resist the wisdom and the spirit by which he spake*[2]. We cannot agree with those who affirm that St. Paul erred[3] when writing to the Thessalonians, and that he " entertained and expressed a belief which the event did not justify," namely, that the Day of the Lord would come while he himself was still alive.

Such assertions as these have been confidently repeated, but have not been proved.

This is the declaration of the Apostles. Not only the *Writers* of Holy Scripture are said by them to be *moved by the Holy Ghost*[4], but the *writing* itself, *every*[5] part of the whole *writing*, is described by St. Paul *as inspired by God*. The Book is inspired, and therefore the Scriptures are called *living* oracles[6], and are represented as *speaking*[7], and as endued with *foreknowledge*[8]. The Spirit of God animates them. They are saturated and bathed with Divine Light. They are Light. *Thy Word is a Lamp unto my feet, and a Light unto my paths*[9].

[2] Acts vi. 8—10.
[3] 1 Thess. iv. 15. So Dr. Arnold and "Essays and Reviews," p. 346.
[4] 2 Pet. i. 21.
[5] πᾶσα γραφὴ (*every* Scripture is) θεόπνευστος, divinely inspired. 2 Tim. iii. 16.
[6] Acts vii. 38.
[7] Mark xv. 28. John xix. 37. Rom. iv. 3; ix. 17; xi. 2. Gal. iv. 30.
[8] Gal. iii. 8.   [9] Ps. cxix. 105.

admission that there are Errors in the Word of God.

We know that the Bible is *for all;* it is for the simplest peasant as well as for the wisest philosopher; it is able to make all men *wise unto salvation*[1]. We cannot admit that the Bible is blemished with errors, and that it is left for the reader "to separate by his own skill" what is erroneous in it from what is true. We know that an unbeliever may justly challenge theologians who make such an admission as that; and that he may fairly encounter them with the following language[2]: "A book cannot be said to be inspired, or to carry with it the authority of being God's Word, if *only portions* come from Him, and there exists *no plain and infallible sign to indicate which* those portions are; and if the same Writer may give us in one verse of the Bible a *revelation from the Most High,* and in the next verse a *blunder of his own.* How can we be certain, that the very texts, upon which we rest our *doctrines* and our *hopes,* are not the *uninspired* portion? What can be the meaning or nature of an Inspiration to teach Truth, which does not guarantee its recipient from teaching error?"

4. In answer to such questions as these, we affirm that the Bible is the Word of God, and that it *is not* marred by human infirmities. We do not imagine with some that the Bible is like a Threshing-floor, on which wheat and chaff lie

---

[1] 2 Tim. iii. 15.

[2] These words are quoted from a Volume entitled the "Creed of Christendom," published by a sceptical writer.

mingled together, and that it is left for the readers of the Bible—simple peasants and young children—to winnow and sift the wheat from the chaff by the fan and sieve of their own intellects. We do not suppose that the Bible is like a rude mass, having threads and spangles of precious metal, intertwisted and encrusted in a mineral bed, and that it is the duty of those who take the Bible into their hands to smelt the ore from the dross. But we believe the Bible to *be pure gold*. *Every word of God is pure*[3]. We adopt the words of one of the wisest divines, S. Augustine[4],—" Such is the reverence I have learnt to pay to the Books of Holy Scripture, and to those Books alone, that I *most firmly believe* that *none* of those Writers *has ever fallen into any error in writing;* and if I find any thing in Scripture which *seems to me at variance with the truth*, I conclude that either *my copy* of the Bible is in fault, or that the translator has

---

[3] Prov. xxx. 5. Cp. Ps. xii. 6; cxix. 140.
[4] *S. Augustine*, Epist. ad Hieron. 82; cp. *S. Irenæus* iii. 1, and iii. 5, where he speaks of the Apostles as having perfect knowledge (perfectam agnitionem) and placed beyond the reach of all falsehood (extrà omne mendacium), and so *Origen* (in Matth. tom. xvi. c. 12), " I believe that not a jot or a tittle of the Gospels is without divine instruction; and that the Gospels were written with the co-operation of the Holy Ghost, and that they who wrote them never fell into an error." See also his Comment on John vi. c. 18; and Homil. in Num. xxvii. 1, where he says that in Holy Scripture there is 'nihil otiosum,' and (Homil. in Jerem. xxxix.), "there is nothing in Scripture which does not do its own proper work, it men know how to use it."

missed the sense, or that I have not rightly understood it[5]."

5. Theologians who imagine that they can maintain the Inspiration of the Bible, and yet assert that the Bible is blemished by errors may be desired to consider, that if the Holy Ghost, Who inspired the Scriptures, had not intended to preserve their writers from error, He would *not* have employed such persons as He did in writing the Scriptures. He would *not* have chosen *unlearned and ignorant men*[6]; but He would have chosen the wise of this world to write the Bible. He would *not* have chosen a Galilæan fisherman, a hundred years old, for such St. John was, to write the evangelic record of the sublimest discourses of Jesus Christ. And if that Galilæan fisherman, and his brother Evangelists, being such as they were, had not been preserved from error by the Holy Ghost, according to Christ's promise, that the Comforter would *teach them all things* and *guide them into all truth,* and *bring all things to their remembrance whatsoever He had said to them* (John xiv. 26; xvi. 13), they must have fallen into countless errors, and manifest contradictions. But the Holy Spirit wisely made choice of feeble instruments, in order that by the weakness of the instruments, and by the perfection of the work done by their means, it might be

[5] See also *Hooker's* judgement on this subject in his Eccles. Polity, II. viii. 6.
[6] Acts iv. 13.

seen and acknowledged by all, that the excellency of the Gospel written by their hands is *not of man, but of God*[7].

6. But while we thus affirm, that the Bible—by which we mean the *genuine text* of the *divine original*—is free from error, we do not mean to assert that *the persons,* who were employed to write the Bible, as Moses, the Prophets, and Apostles, were not liable to err. As *Writers*, they were guided *in writing,* and were preserved from error by the Spirit of Truth, Who inspired them; but, as *men,* they were fallible *in practice.* They confess this. *We are men of like passions with you*[8]. *In many things we offend all*[9]. The unerring Word of God records the errors of the *men,* by whose instrumentality the Word of God was written. Moses relates his own sin for which he was excluded from Canaan: and the Scripture says that he *spake unadvisedly with his lips*[1]. David the Psalmist laments the sins of David the King[2]. St. Luke in the Acts relates that the Evangelist St. Mark faltered for a season, and that St. Paul strove with St. Barnabas concerning him[3]. The unerring language of the Holy Spirit, writing by St. Paul in Holy Scripture, relates that St. Peter erred and *walked not uprightly*[4].

---

[7] 2 Cor. iv. 7. Cp. *Euseb.* Demonst. Evang. iii. 5. Hist. Eccl. iii. 24.
[8] Acts xiv. 15.
[9] James iii. 2.
[1] Deut. xxxii. 51. Ps. cvi. 33.
[2] Ps. li.
[3] Acts xx. 37—39.
[4] Gal. ii. 11—14.

We believe that St. Peter erred, because the Holy Spirit, who cannot err, asserts by St. Paul in Scripture that he did err[5]. But let us not confound the *Writers* with the *men*. And let us distinguish the *Writings* from the *practice* of those by whose hands they were written. Men they were, and being men, though holy men, they were liable to err. But the *Writings* which God the HOLY GHOST dictated by their instrumentality, and which have *been received* as *Holy Scripture* by the *Christian Church Universal*, which is the *Body of Christ, the Pillar and Ground of truth,* are exempt from error. And why? Because in writing they had the gift of the Holy Ghost, who taught them *all things* and *guided them into all truth.*[6] And their words were not such as *man's wisdom teacheth, but which the Holy Ghost teacheth*[7]; and, as St. Peter says, they *spake being moved by the Holy Ghost*[8]; and the Holy Ghost *is the Spirit of truth*[9], and *every Scripture*[1], St. Paul declares, is *given by inspiration of God.* The workmen were human, but the work is divine. They had the *treasure* in *earthen vessels*[2], but the *treasure* itself is *not earthly,* but heavenly. The Channels, *through* which the pure water of Holy Scripture flows, are like the aqueducts of brick stretching across the Roman Campagna,

---

[5] This is clearly stated by S. *Augustine* in his correspondence with S. Jerome, Epist. xxviii. xl. and lxxxii.

[6] John xiv. 26 ; xvi. 13.   [7] 1 Cor. ii. 13.

[8] 2 Pet. i. 21.   [9] John xiv. 17 ; xv. 26.

[1] πᾶσα γραφή, *every* Scripture (2 Tim. iii. 16).

[2] 2 Cor. iv. 7.

but the Water itself, which flows through them, is living water of salvation, streaming forth from the heavenly Hills, even from the pure well-spring of the Wisdom and Love of God.

7. Here also we may advert to those who allege that the language of the Apostles is not from God, because they sometimes speak *doubtingly*. We cannot concur in that statement. And why? Because *Inspiration is not Omniscience;* and *doubt is not error*. The Holy Spirit did not change the human writers into Divine beings. His aid was given to the Writers of Scripture according to the need. Sometimes it swelled the sails of their minds with a vehement gale; and at other times, when the oars of human toil, and the pilotage of human prudence, nearly sufficed for the purpose, would fan them only with a gentle breeze; sometimes it was almost lulled. He allowed the Evangelists to speak *doubtingly* in Scripture in some minor matters, where doubt was not hurtful; such as, for instance, in the capacity of the vessels of Cana[3], or in the number of furlongs which the Apostles had rowed[4]. He allowed St. Paul to avow, that whether he was in the body or out of the body, when he was caught up into the third heaven, he *could not tell*[5]; and to say that he *knows not* whether he baptized any besides those whom he mentions[6]; and He permitted him to express,

---

[3] John ii. 6.
[4] John vi. 19. Cp. xi. 18. Acts iv. 4. Luke ix. 28.
[5] 2 Cor. xii. 2.   [6] 1 Cor. i. 16.

doubts concerning the future [7]. He inspired them to *inform* us of *their doubts* in these cases, in order that, in those other more momentous and mysterious matters, wherein *they express no doubt*, we may feel sure that they do not speak from themselves, but from God.

8. Again. Doubtless there is a *perfect language* in *heaven*. But we may not allow ourselves to forget, that when God communicated the mysteries of Revelation to the world, in the pages of Holy Scripture, He did not speak in the tongues of Angels, nor did He create any new language, but He used a language already in being, a language formed by the ordinary intercourse of man with man, a language spoken in senates and law-courts, and streets and market-places of the world. Writing to men He used the language of men. *The medium* by which He revealed the mysteries of the Gospel, was *ancient* and *human*, but what He revealed thereby was *new* and *Divine*.

It is with Scripture as with Christ's Tribute-money [8]. The metallic ore, of which that money was made, was from God, it was dug up in the mine; and Christ by His miraculous power brought up the sum paid, from the depths of the sea: but the Coin itself, in which the sum was paid, had been struck in Cæsar's mint. So the substance of Scripture-Doctrine is from God. Its mysteries

---

[7] Rom. xv. 24. 1 Cor. xvi. 5, 6. 2 Cor. i. 15—17. Phil. ii. 19. 1 Tim. iii. 14.

[8] Matt. xvii. 24—27.

are brought up from the abysses of Divine Wisdom. The words in which they are revealed, are words employed by God, through the ministry of inspired men. But the language, of which those words form a part, was framed by man; it was struck in a human mint; and like every thing made by the hand of man, that language was not free from imperfection; though doubtless the words, when used by men under the guidance of God, serve perfectly all the purposes, which God, in using them, *intended them* to serve. Almighty God did not destroy the writers' identity, He did not annul their free-will, but He used the writers aright. He did not create a new language, but He used the old with Divine Wisdom and Truth.

9. One more prefatory observation may be made here.

It is sometimes alleged, that since the collation of the different Manuscripts of the Old and New Testament has brought to light an immense multitude of *Various Readings*, amounting to some hundreds of thousands, therefore, in this diversity of authorities, even *if* an inspired Text, and faultless Original, did exist any where, it would be impossible for us to find it out.

As to this objection from the multitude of Various Readings, this is *not* an *evidence* of *uncertainty* in the Sacred Text, but it is rather a proof of its *certainty*. The words of the original Scripture have been transcribed by human copyists, and though it is certain that no single copy, now existing, either of the Old or New Testament in their original tongues, exhibits precisely verbatim et literatim what was written by the Prophets and Apostles, yet it is also certain that, by *collation* of the copies which have been preserved, we have the Text of the Holy Scriptures in such a form, as may be depended on for all that we require, and that, in receiving that Text, we receive the Oracles of God.

For, let us consider; Whence does this *multitude of Various Readings arise?* From the *multitude of copies.* And this multitude of copies is the very thing which secures and proves the integrity of the Text. *If* we had only *a few* copies, there would be few Various Readings; and *if* there was only *one* copy, there would be *no* Various Readings at all. But then we should only have one witness to depend upon. But now we have many thousand witnesses, and since these witnesses *do vary* in some *very slight, trivial,* and *insignificant* matters, such as the omission of a word, or its transposition, or in a particle or conjunction, we see that there is no collusion, no conspiracy among the witnesses. And since they *agree in all substantial* respects, we are sure that their *witness is true,* and that the Text, obtained by their aid, is correct; that it is a faithful representation for all needful purposes, of the Words dictated to the Prophets, Apostles, and Evangelists, by the Holy Spirit of God.

III. Let us now proceed to suppose that an *unbeliever* were to address us, and ask for a *reason of the hope* that is in us, when we assert our belief that the Bible is the Word of God.

What answer should we give to that question?

If that belief is sound, there must be a *reason* for it. And since the Bible is *for all*—for the poor as well as rich, for the simple as well as the learned—and all are bound to believe its doctrines and obey its precepts, it is clear that the answer to be given to this question ought to be of such a kind, that *all*, however unlearned, may be *able* to *give* it, and that all to whom it is given ought to be satisfied with it.

Suppose therefore that an unbeliever were to ask you this question. "On what grounds do you believe the Bible to be the Word of God?"

1. Some persons have said, in reply to this inquiry, that *they themselves* have an *inward spiritual illumination*, by which they are enabled to discern the Bible to be God's Word. The Spirit *in their hearts*, they affirm, bears witness to the Spirit in the Bible, and assures them that it is His Word.

We do not deny the force of this answer in due measure and degree. But is it *adequate?* Is it satisfactory?

Doubtless every devout person will feel, in reading the Bible, that he is reading no common book; he *will feel his heart burn within him* (Luke xxiv. 32), with holy love and joy, when he listens to its words, and when he observes the harmony of the various parts of the Bible, and its adaptation to the needs of our nature, and the fulfilment of its prophecies; and when he reflects on the moral and social benefits conferred by the Bible on the world; and when he meditates on the wonderful dispensations of God's providence in protecting and preserving the Bible [9]. Every one who is enlightened with divine grace will feel a strong persuasion that it *is* the Word of God.

2. But such considerations as these, important as they are, would not *suffice to convince an unbeliever* that the Bible is the Word of God. We need some *other* aid. It cannot be truly said by any man, that, if portions of the Bible were interspersed with portions of an uninspired book, —such as the Book of Ecclesiasticus or of Wisdom, —and if, being thus blended together, they were placed before him, he could, by his own *internal consciousness*, discern and separate what is inspired from what is uninspired [1].

---

[9] This is enlarged upon below, Lecture V.

[1] *Hooker* says well on this point (Eccl. Pol. III. viii. 15):—"I doubt not but men of wisdom and judgment will grant, that the Church, in this point especially (the *Inspiration* of Holy Scripture), is furnished with reason, to stop the mouths of her impious adversaries; and that as it were *altogether bootless to allege against them* what the Spirit had taught *us*, so likewise that even to our own selves it needeth caution and explication how the testimony of the Spirit may be discerned, by what means it may be known; lest men think that the Spirit of *God* doth testify those things which the spirit of *error* suggesteth."

And *Bishop Burnet* (on the VIth Article) judiciously observes;

22 *Private Consciousness no safe ground for belief in the Inspiration of the Bible.*

We do well to believe the Inspiration of the Bible. But let those who would build their belief upon *their own feelings,* in this momentous matter, be entreated to consider, whether they may not be building on the sand, and whether they do not need more solid arguments to persuade *others.* Strong *reasons* are requisite to convince the *unbeliever* that the *whole Bible is the Word of God:* he will not be satisfied with assertions, he will require *proofs.* *Our* perceptions are no rule for *him.* He will not ask for emotions, but evidences; he will require, not feelings, but facts. He may say to us, " *You* feel that the Bible is inspired, but *I* have no such feeling; and why should *I* be guided by *your* feelings in *receiving* the Bible, rather than *you* be swayed by *my* feelings in *rejecting* it? Besides, if I am to be influenced by men's feelings, I should have as many different Bibles as there are different Religions. The Brahmin will tell me that he feels a divine spirit speaking to him

In proof of the Inspiration of Holy Scripture "I will not urge that of the testimony of the Spirit, which many have had recourse to: this is only an argument to him that feels it, if it is one at all; and therefore it proves *nothing to another person;* besides, the utmost that with reason can be made of this is, that a good man feeling the very powerful effects of the Christian religion on his own heart, in the reforming his nature, and the calming his conscience, together with those comforts that arise out of it, is convinced in general of the whole of Christianity, by the happy effects that it has upon his own mind; but it does not from this appear, how he should know that *such books and such passages in them should come from a Divine original.* or that he *should be able to distinguish what is genuine in them from what is spurious.*"

in the Vedas; the Mahometan thinks that he hears a divine voice in the Koran; the Jew, who recognizes a divine presence in the Old Testament, denies its existence in the New. And even among Christians, some [2] receive the Apocryphal Books, such as the Books of Judith and Tobit, as divinely inspired, while others [3] do not own them as such. *If* personal feelings and opinions, apart from logical proofs, are to determine the matter, every form of Religion may have a separate Bible, and there can be no common standard, no uniform Rule of Faith and Practice for all."

3. Consider, also, to what disastrous results this reference to private feelings and opinions in the question of Inspiration, has already led.

That theory was put forth by some pious men at the Reformation in the sixteenth century. To cite one of the greatest names of that time—Martin Luther said that he himself could not reconcile the doctrine of St. James with that of St. Paul, on the subject of Justification, and that *therefore*, inasmuch as he accepted the doctrine of St. Paul, he must reject the Epistle of St. James, which he called "an Epistle of straw." In a similar temper he rejected the Book of Revelation of St. John the Divine. He did not *feel* their Inspiration; they were not congenial to *his* opinions; they did not approve themselves to his mind. The Apostle St. Paul was inspired, *because*

---

[2] Members of the Church of Rome. Concil. Trident. Sess. iv.
[3] The Church of England, Art. VI.

Martin Luther felt his inspiration! But the Apostles St. James and St. John were to wait for an allowance of their Inspiration till the feelings of Martin Luther should change! There is reason to believe that Luther lived long enough to rue this rash and reckless presumption [4]. But this example of arbitrary wilfulness, in dealing with Holy Scripture, did great mischief. Other Reformers, and even entire Reformed Churches [5],—happily *not* the Church of England [6],—grounded their recognition of Holy Scripture, and their belief in its Inspiration, upon the *foundation alone* of what they called the *internal witness* of the Spirit in themselves. They resolved their belief into a mere private intuition, and personal assurance in their own hearts. They made themselves the judges of God's Word.

Here was the root of the evil which has now grown up into a tree and overshadows Europe with darkness, and blights the vegetation beneath it, and yields deadly fruit; as may be seen in "Essays and Reviews," and (I deeply regret to add) in Bishop Colenso's and Dean Stanley's writings on the Old Testament. They who rested their belief in the Bible on such a basis as that, were unable to defend the Bible against those who assailed it. Their belief in the Bible was true, but it rested on false grounds. It was built on

---

[4] See *Gerhardi* Loci Theol. Appendix de Scr. Sacrâ, § 279 and § 299.   [5] Confessio Belgica v. Confessio Gallicana iv.
[6] See below, Lecture IV.

the shifting quicksand of private opinion. As long as men *agreed* in feeling that inner Consciousness which led them to acknowledge the Truth and Inspiration of the Bible, so long the unsoundness of the foundation did not manifestly appear. But they were dwelling in a tottering house; and ere long the storm came, and the house fell. Persons arose after them, who appealed to their own Consciousness, as a sufficient reason for *rejecting* portions of the Bible. And they who had received the Bible on the assurance of their own supposed inner illumination, were unable to give any reply to those who *rejected* it on similar grounds. The inner Consciousness of the one party was set against the inner Consciousness of the other party. . . . And who could arbitrate between them?

4. Thus in looking back to the history of Christendom, we see that the erroneous principle which was adopted by some pious men, *in support of the Bible*, three centuries ago, has now been applied by others *to destroy the Bible*.

Some recently published Volumes, contravening the truth and inspiration of Scripture, which have startled the religious mind of the English Public, are only the natural fruit of the waywardness of private opinion developed in a sceptical direction. They have brought to the surface what has long been lurking beneath it. But if we are not wanting to ourselves, great good may be the result.

Relying on what they call "the verifying

faculty" in their own minds, some impugn the veracity and genuineness of the Pentateuch, because they *think* that its records are inconsistent with the results of scientific research, or because they *suppose* its language to be posterior to the age of Moses. Some reject the Book of Daniel, because they *imagine* that its Prophecies were subsequent to the events which it professes to predict. Others will not receive the second Epistle of St. Peter, because the style of that Epistle differs from the First, and because they *think* that both those Epistles could not have been written by the same Author.[7] In short, there is scarcely a single book in the Bible, which has not now been called into question by men who are swayed by their own feelings, and biassed by their own private opinions. "The nature of the Inspiration of Scripture," they say, "can only be shown from the examination of Scripture[8]," and whatever they find in the Bible *congenial to themselves,* whatever harmonizes with *their own sentiments, that* they believe to be inspired, and *that alone.* Thus the divinity of the Bible is made to depend on the fickleness of human caprice;

---

[7] See *Hävernick's* Einleitung in das Alte Testament, 1836—1849, and *Guerike's* Einleitung in das N. T., 1843.

[8] "Essays and Reviews," p. 347. And again, "to the question, 'What is inspiration?' the first answer is, 'The idea which *we gather* from the study of it.' This is reconcileable with *variations* in *fact* in the Gospels . . . with *inaccuracies of language* in the Epistles of St. Paul."

and "unless God pleases man He is to be no longer God[9]."

The Genuineness and Inspiration of the Bible as a whole being thus made matter of doubt, the Bible itself is to be no longer the standard of Faith and Practice, but the varying consciousness of the individual is to be substituted in the place of God's Holy Word.

There can be no uniform standard of *Interpretation*, upon such principles as these. The Bible becomes like a "leaden rule," which men may bend aside according to their own will[1]. And thus they fall under St. Peter's censure, who says that *they that are unlearned and unstable wrest the Scriptures to their own destruction*[2].

IV. This condition of things is fraught with warning and instruction. It teaches us that it is not enough to believe the truth, but that it is necessary to believe it on *right grounds*. If Belief is made to rest on a wrong foundation, it must give rise to Unbelief. It is not enough to believe that the Bible is God's written Word, but it is necessary to be able to *convince others* that this proposition is true. It is necessary (as St. Peter affirms) to

---

[9] Nisi homini Deus placuerit, Deus non erit.—*Tertullian*, Apol. c. 5.

[1] Or, in the language of *Dryden*,
  "Their airy faith will no foundation find;
  The Word's a *weathercock to every wind.*"

[2] 2 Pet. iii. 16.

be *always ready to give to every man* that *asketh* us a *reason of the hope that is in us.*

Let us examine ourselves, whether we are able to do this. Let those who have hitherto built their belief on the basis of private feelings and opinions, be earnestly entreated to contemplate the superstructure of error, which has now risen up upon that basis. Let them be desired to reconsider their principles. The prevalence of Infidelity among us, the avowal of strange doctrines concerning the Inspiration of the Bible, which is the groundwork of all our hopes, imperatively demand this at our hands.

England is now on her trial. Now is the crisis of her religious life. If she has strength to eject the poison which has been infused into her, she may become more vigorous than before. But if not, that poison will curdle in her veins, and her system will be diseased, and a moral mortification will ensue; and England will be in a few years, what some other Nations of Europe now are.

Let us consider calmly the signs of the times; let us endeavour, by God's grace, to maintain the truth; let us charitably and wisely labour to overcome evil with good. Then we may be sure, that the dangers, by which the Faith is now assailed, will be occasions of new victories. Our difficulties are God's opportunities. Our midnight is His noon. Our trials may be our triumphs. They may conduce to heal our unhappy differences and dissensions, and to unite us all in the truth.

If the Bible is the unerring word of the Everliving God; if, as we believe, it is the Rule of Faith and Practice; if it is the Charter of our social and national privileges upon earth, and of our everlasting citizenship in heaven; if it is the Code, by which we shall be judged at the Great Day; then we may be sure, that all attacks upon it will one day recoil upon those who make them, like the foam and spray dashed from the firm-set rock.

The violence of the storm will prove the strength of the fortress, and will confirm our belief in its impregnability, and in the faithfulness and power of Him, whose Divine Eye is ever upon it, and who shields it with the defence of His own Almighty protection. And thus, though the sea around us is tempestuous, *and though the waters thereof rage and swell*, yet in His own appointed time the *rivers of the flood thereof will make glad the city of God*[3].

What is the *true foundation* on which the belief of the Inspiration of Holy Scripture is to be built? and what are the reasons by which we may hope to convince others, that the Bible, the whole Bible, and nothing but the Bible, is the written Word of God?

These questions will be considered in the following lectures. Let me entreat your prayers for God's help in this work, for His honour and glory, through Jesus Christ our Lord. Amen.

[3] Ps. xlvi. 2, 3.

LECTURE II.

Romans iii. 1, 2.

What advantage then hath the Jew? Much every way: chiefly, because that unto them were committed the Oracles of God.

I. 1. In the last lecture we entered on the inquiry,

"By what reasons are we persuaded, and by what arguments would we persuade others, that the Bible is the Word of God?"

It was then observed, that some persons have replied to this question by saying, that they have an inward illumination, by which they are enabled to distinguish the Bible from all other books; and they rest their belief in the Inspiration of the Bible upon this private assurance.

But, as was then remarked, this assurance on *their* part cannot exercise any influence on *others*. *Our* belief in the Inspiration of the Bible cannot induce an *unbeliever* to receive it as God's Word.

It has also been already shown, that this appeal

to private feelings and opinions, as the groundwork of belief in the Bible, has led to unhappy results. If we refer to our own feelings and opinions as an adequate proof of its Inspiration, we must not be surprised to find that other persons refer to *their* feelings and opinions, in *disproof* of it.

2. It is hardly necessary to say, that we cannot prove from *Scripture itself* alone, that Scripture is God's Word. The Holy Spirit says by St. Paul, that *all Scripture is given by Inspiration of God*[1]. But it must *first* be *proved* by arguments *external* to Scripture, as well as by *internal* evidence derivable from Scripture, that St. Paul himself, when he wrote these words, wrote under the Inspiration of God[2].

II. Let us now open the OLD TESTAMENT, and let us proceed to enquire on what grounds are we convinced, and by what proofs would we endeavour to persuade others, that the Old Testament is the Word of God?

[1] 2 Tim. iii. 16.
[2] See *Hooker*, I. xiv. 1. "Of things necessary, the very chiefest is to know what books we are bound to *esteem holy;* which point is *confessed impossible for Scripture* itself to teach." And again, II. iv. 2, " It is not the Word of God which doth or possibly can assure us that we do well to think that *is* His Word ; for if any one Book of Scripture did give testimony to all, yet still *that* Scripture would require another to give credit to it; nor could we ever come to any pause to rest our assurance this way ; so that unless *beside Scripture* there were something that might assure us that we do well, we could not think we do well, no not in being assured that Scripture is a sacred and holy rule of well-doing."

1. First, we would reply, we receive the Old Testament as inspired, on the testimony of God, declared in the consent and practice of the Jewish Nation, to which "*were delivered*[3] *the Oracles of God.*" The Ancient Jewish Church was the divinely constituted Recipient and Guardian of the Old Testament. Its testimony on this matter is the testimony of God.

2. Secondly, we receive the Old Testament as inspired, on the testimony of the Son of God, our Blessed Lord and Saviour JESUS CHRIST.

3. Thirdly, we receive the Old Testament as inspired, on the testimony of God the HOLY GHOST, testifying to its truth and inspiration, by the mouth of the Holy Apostles, and by the *consent* of the Christian Church, to which our Blessed Lord promised to send the Holy Spirit "*to teach her all things,*" and to "*guide her into all truth, and to abide with her for ever*[4]."

First, then, we receive the Old Testament as inspired, on the testimony of Almighty God, declared by the Jewish Nation.

III. Here we must begin by showing that the Old Testament, as it now exists in *our* age, is *the*

---

[3] St. Paul's words are ἐπιστεύθησαν τὰ λόγια, a stronger phrase than that in our English Version. "They were *entrusted with* the oracles of God." The Jews were the Trustees and Guardians of the Old Testament; and our Lord and His Apostles acknowledged that they were faithful to their trust, in guarding it from alteration.   [4] John xvi. 7. 13; xiv. 26.

Integrity of the Text of the Old Testament, how secured, and proved.

same as the Old Testament in the first century of the Christian era: in other words, we must prove its *integrity*, or *identity*.

Its *identity* may be proved from the fact, that the Old Testament has been *publicly read* both in Jewish Synagogues [5], and in Christian Churches [6], throughout the world, every week, from the first century after Christ to the present day.

The *multiplication* of copies of the Old Testament, for the purposes of this weekly public Reading in the Jewish Synagogues on the Jewish Sabbath, and in Christian Churches on the Lord's Day, and this public Reading itself, have served as providential guarantees for the *preservation* of the Old Testament.

Even *if any* of the Jews had ever desired to tamper with the Text of the Old Testament, they would have been prevented from effecting such a purpose by the diffusion of copies of the Old Testament—in the *original* Hebrew and in *Translations* of it—such as the Chaldee, Syriac, and the Septuagint or Greek Version, and the Ancient Latin Versions, and others [7]. Even *if all* the *Jewish* Synagogues had conspired together to alter the Text of the Old Testament, which is a thing incredible,

---

[5] See on Acts xiii. 15; xv. 21. *Josephus* c. Apion. ii. p. 1072, and the authorities in *Vitringa's* treatise De Synagogâ Vetere, lib. iii. pt. ii. c. 8, p. 961, ed. Franck. 1696.

[6] See the authorities in *Bingham's* Antiquities, book xiv. ch. iii.

[7] See *S. Augustine's* observation on this point, De Civitate Dei, xv. c. 13.

they would have been hindered and checked from doing so by the counteracting vigilance of *Christian* Churches, guarding the Old Testament, and publicly reading the Old Testament in all parts of the civilized world.

And *if*, on the other side, any *Christian* Churches had ever attempted to make any change in the Old Testament, such an attempt would have been exposed and frustrated by the *Jews*.

Thus we see, that under God's providential care for the Old Testament, even the enmity of Jews and Christians has been overruled for good; it has been made instrumental in the preservation of His Holy Word, and in assuring the world of its integrity.

A Poet of old, speaking of a ship in a stormy night, says, "that in such a time it is good to have *two Anchors* cast out of the vessel," one anchor from the prow, the other at the stern, in order that it may ride safely in the storm[b]. In the tempests of the long night of many centuries, the sacred vessel of Holy Scripture has been moored securely on the two Anchors of the Jewish Synagogue and of the Christian Church.

It is certain that the Old Testament, as it is now in the hands of the Jews dispersed every where, coincides with the Old Testament in the hands of the Christian Churches diffused throughout the world.

This coincidence is a proof, that the Old Testa-

[b] *Pindar*, Olymp. vi. 172.

With what reverence the Jews in our Lord's age regarded the Old Testament?

ment, which *we* have in *our* hands *at this day*, is the *same* as the Old Testament in the first century of the Christian era.

IV. Let us, therefore, now ascend in our thoughts to the first century of the Christian era, and imagine ourselves living then; and suppose the case of pious Israelites, such, for example, as an aged Simeon or a guileless Nathanael at that time.

By what arguments would the religious Jews of that age have been persuaded, and by what evidence would they have sought to persuade others, that the Old Testament which they had, is *inspired* by God?

1. Doubtless the first motive which impelled the devout Israelite to acknowledge the Old Testament as divine, was the fact that he saw it set apart from all other Books by the universal consent and uniform practice of his own Nation, to which God had vouchsafed wonderful marks of His favour and blessing.

He saw the Books of the Old Testament treated with pious reverence by the whole Hebrew people. He beheld those Books treasured up with devout care in the Synagogues, and brought forth, Sabbath after Sabbath, from the sacred chest in those Synagogues; he saw those Volumes unveiled and unrolled with holy veneration; and before and after the reading of those Writings, he heard the accents of blessing and praise addressed to God for the gift of those sacred Writings, and he listened to their words recited with scrupulous care, and venerated with religious awe [9].

Every Jew, from his infancy, was thus impressed with a belief in the Truth and Inspiration of the Old Testament.

2. The feelings with which the pious Israelite regarded the Old Testament are thus described by a Writer living in the Apostolic age, who was eminently qualified to bear witness on this subject. That person is Josephus, the Jewish Historian, one of the most learned Authors of that time, a Pharisee, and of a priestly family, and descended from the Asmonean Princes. He speaks of the Old Testament as follows:[1] "We have not a multitude of books at variance with one another," as the Heathen have, "but we have only Twenty-two Books:" (such was the reckoning of the Jews, by whom several Books of the Old Testament were counted as one; for instance, the Twelve Minor Prophets were reckoned by them as one Book [2], and so, on the whole, their Twenty-two Books, beginning with Genesis and ending with Malachi, correspond to *our* Books of the Old Testament.) "We have only Twenty-two Books, which contain

---

[9] The Jewish authorities, describing the forms and ceremonies used in the Synagogues, at the reading of the Old Testament, may be seen in the Treatise of *Vitringa*, De Synagogâ Vetere, lib. iii. pt. ii. cap. 8, pp. 961—975. See also the account of the reading of the Old Testament in the Synagogues, in *Dean Prideaux's Connexion*, part i. book vi. on B.C. 445—433.

[1] *Josephus* c. Apion. i. § 8.

[2] See *Bp. Cosin* on the Canon of Scripture, chap. ii.

the record of all time, and are *the Books* which are rightly *believed to be divine*. Five of these are the Books of Moses, which comprise our Laws, and the history of the human race until the death of Moses."

Josephus then proceeds to describe the other Books of the Old Testament; and sums up his account with these memorable words;—" We show by our practice, what our belief is as to these Books. For, although so long a time has elapsed since they were written, yet *no one has ever ventured to make any addition to them, or to take any thing from them, or to make any change in them.* And it is a principle innate in every Jew, to *regard these Books as Oracles of God, and to cleave to them; yea, and to die gladly for them.*"

Such, then, was the judgment of the Jewish Nation concerning the Old Testament.

V. On what proofs did this judgment rest? How was the Jewish Nation convinced that the Old Testament in its hands was *genuine* and had not been tampered with and adulterated?

How was it persuaded that it is *true?*

How was it satisfied that it is *inspired by God?*

1. First, (as was before observed) the Diffusion of those Books into all parts of the world, and the weekly public Reading of them for many centuries in Synagogues before the Christian era, had secured their *identity*. The Translation also of those Books into the Greek language [3], and the

[3] See *Josephus*, Antiquities xii. 2. 4—15.

multiplication of copies in that language was another safeguard which preserved them from being altered or tampered with. The formation of Chaldee Paraphrases of the Old Testament served also for a similar purpose.

2. Even the greatest national *afflictions* of the Hebrew People had been made by God to subserve His gracious purposes in guarding, preserving, and disseminating His own Word, and in assuring the world of its Integrity.

In the age of King Rehoboam, the son of Solomon, Ten Tribes of Israel had revolted from the House of Judah [4], and they always remained separate from the Two Tribes of Judah and Benjamin. Israel and Judah were split asunder, and formed two rival kingdoms. This was a great calamity, but God educed *good* from it: the one Kingdom acted as a check on the other in the custody of the Bible. Though these kingdoms were *opposed* to each other in other respects, yet they *agreed* in receiving the *same Bible*. Thus under God they co-operated in the guardianship of His Word.

If King Jeroboam and his successors on the Throne of Israel, and the Ten Tribes who were subject to them, had been able to convict the Two Tribes of making any alteration in the Old Testament they would not have failed to do so. The Kings of Israel, after its defection from Judah, set up *rival objects of worship* at Dan and Beersheba; and they would have drawn off more

---

[4] 1 Kings xii. 16—19.

worshippers from Jerusalem to their own altars, and have strengthened their own secular power, if they could have alleged with truth that the Two Tribes had been faithless to their trust, and had tampered with the Word of God. And *if*, on *their* side, the *Ten Tribes* had made any change in the text of the Old Testament, the *Two Tribes* would have raised their protest against such alteration.

The fact however is, that the Ten Tribes and the Two Tribes, though severed from each other by many religious jealousies, and political antipathies, had *one and the same Bible*. Though *Ephraim envied Judah, and Judah vexed Ephraim* [5], yet Ephraim and Judah *agreed* in receiving and revering the same Scriptures. And though in course of time the Ten Tribes were carried away captive [6] beyond the Euphrates, and were scattered abroad in Media and Persia, and also in Asia and Egypt; and though afterwards the Two Tribes also were taken away [7] from their own home to Babylon and to other cities of the East, yet all *the Twelve Tribes*, wherever dispersed throughout the world, were *united* as one man in the *reading* of the *same Scriptures;* and they have maintained that union inviolate even to this hour [8].

[5] Isa. xi. 13.   [6] 2 Kings xvii. 6.
[7] 2 Kings xxiv. 10; xxv. 11. 20.
[8] The case of the Samaritan Pentateuch affords no exception to this statement. The Samaritans were foreigners (see Luke xvii. 18, and cp. *Hengstenberg*, Die Authentie des Pentateuches, p. 4), and not Israelites. And the general agreement of the Samaritan Pentateuch with the Hebrew affords a testimony to the

3. This universal *reception* and *public reading* of the Old Testament by the *Jewish Nation* is also a proof of its historical *Truth*.

Consider the contents of the Old Testament. Open the Bible. Examine the Pentateuch, or five Books of Moses. They do *not* give a *flattering* representation of the Hebrew Nation. On the contrary, they exhibit it in a very *unfavourable light*. They display the Israelites as rebelling against God immediately after they had been rescued from Egypt, and when He was doing mighty works in their behalf, and showering down favours upon them. *If*, as some allege, the Author of the Pentateuch had endeavoured to palm upon the Hebrew Nation a fictitious account of mercies that had never been vouchsafed to their forefathers, and of miracles that had never been wrought, he would have endeavoured to ingratiate himself with the Nation, by giving a *favourable* picture of the piety and virtue of their ancestors. He would have said that all the People were so astounded by the stupendous majesty of the miracles, and were so affected by the gracious

---

integrity of the latter. See *Bp. Walton*, Prolegomena, cap xi., and *Dr. Bentley* on Freethinking, Remark xxvii. *Dr. McCaul's* Examination of Bp. Colenso, p. 160. The allegation that there are interpolations in the Pentateuch, which are later than the age of Moses, is carefully examined by *Hävernick*, § 134, pp. 541—9 of the original work, or pp 361, 362 of the English Translation, 1850. Cp. *Hengstenberg*, Die Authentie des Pentateuches, vol. ii. pp. 179—338.

beneficence of the mercies, that they were riveted by them in unswerving obedience.

But no; Moses displays to us the Hebrew Nation as falling into idolatry in the wilderness, after their deliverance from their enemies, and when God was about to give them the Law from Mount Sinai [9]. He exhibits them rebelling against God at the very time when He was feeding them with bread from heaven, and giving them water from the rock [1], and leading them with a pillar of fire [2]. At the close of the forty years' sojourn in the wilderness, just before his death, his testimony of them is, *Thou art a stiff-necked People. Ye have been rebellious against the Lord, from the day that I knew you* [3]. The Pentateuch is a *censure* upon Israel, it is a *condemnation* of the Hebrew Nation for its idolatry and rebellion against God.

Can any man seriously imagine that such a history as this would have been accepted by the Hebrews as *divine, if* it had not been *true?*

The Books of Moses also relate, that on account of their *sins*, all the Israelites that came out of Egypt, with the exception of two, were excluded from the Land of Promise [4]. Thus the Author frankly confesses the insufficiency of his own guidance and government to bring them into that Land, and implies a failure on his part.

[9] Exod. xxxii.
[2] Exod. xiv. 20.
[1] Exod. xvi. 2; and xvii. 2.
[3] Deut. ix. 6, 7. 24. May I be allowed to refer to my notes on this Chapter, which is very important in this light.
[4] Deut. i. 35, 36. 38.

He also records *his own sin,* and his consequent exclusion from Canaan [5]. He relates likewise the sin of his brother Aaron [6] in making the golden calf; and the sin of his sister Miriam [7] in murmuring against himself; and the sin of his brother's sons Nadab and Abihu [8], for which they were destroyed by God; and the sin of some of his own Tribe, Korah and his company, for which they were consumed by fire [9].

Men are prone to speak well of themselves, and to eulogize their own nation. No man is eager to propagate calumnies and perpetuate slanders against himself and his own family, and the people committed to his rule. Nations are wont to dress up their own History in terms flattering to themselves. No Nation in the world has ever adopted libels on itself, and publicly recited them *as true,* and has venerated them as *oracles of God. If* the Books of Moses are not true, the Author of them would have been condemned by the Jews as an impostor and a slanderer of the Nation, and as a blasphemer of God, and his books would have been consigned by them to perpetual infamy.

But the Hebrew People *has* accepted the Pentateuch as *its own* History written *by inspiration of God.* It has publicly read it as such ever since it was written. The great National yearly Festivals

---

[5] Numb. xx. 12.   [6] Exod. xxxii.
[7] Numb. xii. 1.   [8] Levit. x. 1.
[9] Numb. xvi.

to which the Jews resorted from all parts of the world, were standing monuments of the historical veracity of the Pentateuch. The Passover, Pentecost, and Tabernacles, at which the Pentateuch was publicly read in the ears of all the people every seventh year [1], commemorated the wonderful facts, recorded by Moses in the Pentateuch, and bore witness to its truth.

Therefore we may justly conclude that the Pentateuch is historically *true*.

4. The Israelite, being thus convinced of the *Integrity and Truth* of the Pentateuch, would next proceed to consider the proof of its *Inspiration*.

In that *true* History he saw his own Nation set apart by God, from ancient days, as a peculiar People. He knew from that History that the Tabernacle[2] in the wilderness had been fenced off by God from other places. He knew that in that Tabernacle there was a place distinguished from the rest, and called the "*Holy of Holies.*" He knew that in the mysterious darkness of that Holy of Holies, separated by the Veil, which hung before it, was the Ark; and, above the Ark, the Mercy Seat; and on the Mercy Seat the Cherubim, stretching their wings over it; and that this Mercy Seat was the Dwelling-place of God.

5. Observe now the visible and practical testimony thus afforded by God Himself to the *Inspiration* of the Old Testament.

---

[1] Deut. xxxi. 10.   [2] Exod. xxv. 8—22; xxvi. 33.

As soon as the Pentateuch was written, He commanded Moses that it should be placed in the Holy of Holies, by the side of the Ark, the Throne of God[3]. Remember what the Holy of Holies was. It was the type and figure of heaven itself[4]. And into it no one might enter, except the High Priest, and he only once a year. By placing therefore the Pentateuch *there*, God Himself has set apart *that* Book from all other books. He enshrined it in His own Oracle. He consecrated it. The God of Truth Himself thus avouched its veracity. The Omnipotent thus protected it. He received it under *the shadow of His Wings* and made it *safe under His feathers*[5]. The Holy One of Israel proclaimed its sanctity, and acknowledged it as His own.

This book of the Law, treasured up in the Holy of Holies, was the Original from which Copies were to be made; and it was the standard by which those copies were to be revised and verified. The sacred Original was to remain in

---

[3] See Deut. xxxi. 9. 24—26. Josh. xxiv. 26. That this command concerned the whole Pentateuch is shown by *Hävernick*, Einleitung i. p. 19. The objection of some recent sceptical writers (such as *De Wette* and others), alleging that this statement is inconsistent with the assertion in 1 Kings viii. 9, that in Solomon's days there was nothing in the Ark save the Two Tables of stone, is refuted by the fact that the Law is *not* said in Deut. xxxi. 26, to be deposited *in* the Ark, but *by the side* of it. Cp. *Josephus*, Antiq. viii. 4.

[4] Heb. ix. 7—11. *Bp. Pearson* on the Creed, Art. V.

[5] Ps. xci. 4.

Original of the Pentateuch to be copied out by the Kings with their own hand.

the Most Holy Place. But the knowledge of its contents was to be diffused every where.

6. In order still further to declare its *divine authority*, Almighty God commanded that the Kings of the Hebrew Nation, on their accession to the throne, should make with their own hands a copy of the Law from the Original that was kept in the Holy of Holies [6]. Sovereigns were to be its transcribers, and to keep the Law of God always by their side, as the code and charter of their government [7].

This sacred Original was preserved in the Tabernacle, and in the Temple, for many generations [8]; and in all probability it was this Original, which, having been rescued from the hands of idolatrous Princes, and secreted in evil days, was discovered in the Temple, in the days of the good King Josiah [9]. It was the sight of that venerable Volume, written by the great Lawgiver, and the sound of the divine words recited from that holy oracle, which affected the tender heart of that pious youthful Prince with awe and penitential sorrow for the sins of the People committed to his charge, and with godly fear of the divine judgments hanging over their heads.

---

[6] Deut. xvii. 18, 19. Josh. i. 8.

[7] Cp. the remarks of *Hävernick*, Einleitung, § 139 of the original, or § 35 of the English Translation.

[8] See preceding page.

[9] 2 Chron. xxxiv. 14, 15. 2 Kings xxii. 8—10. See *Bishop Patrick* and *Dr. Kennicott* on 2 Kings xxii. 8, and *Hävernick's* Einleitung, § 139, or § 35 of the English Translation.

7. The *Truth* of the *Pentateuch* being proved, and its *Inspiration* being avouched, it follows as a necessary consequence that the *rest of the Old Testament* is also divinely *inspired*.

The Old Testament was called "*the Law, and the Prophets*[1]," and it is certain that all the Jews regarded the *Prophets* as on a par with the *Law*. They revered *the Law and the Prophets* as the lively oracles of God.

Almighty God had commanded in the *Law*, that if any man laid claim to be called a *Prophet* of the Lord, and could not establish that claim, he was to be put to death[2].

Thus God had provided a safeguard against the reception of any prophecy, which could not *prove its divine origin*. And since the *Prophetical Books* of the Old Testament *were received* universally by the Hebrew Nation as of *equal authority* with the Books of the *Law*, which were enshrined by God's command in the Holy of Holies, and since God Himself, Who was the Sovereign of the Nation, did not censure that reception, but approved and sanctioned it, this concurrent consent of God's people is no other than the witness of God Himself to the Divine Authority of the Prophets.

Consider, also, that the Hebrew Prophets do not flatter the Hebrew People. They speak with holy boldness, as Ambassadors of God, in stern and severe language, and rebuke them for their

---

[1] See Matt. xxii. 40. Luke xvi. 16. Acts xiii. 15.
[2] Deut. xiii. 5; xviii. 20. Cp. Jer. xiv. 15. Zech. xiii. 3.

Divine Inspiration of the Prophetical Books of
the Old Testament.

sins, and call them to repentance, and denounce divine retribution upon them, unless they repent. God's commission to them was, *Cry aloud, spare not, lift up thy voice like a trumpet, and show My people their transgression, and the House of Jacob their sins* [3].

Can it be supposed, that the Hebrew People would have received such writings, and would have revered them as of equal authority with the Books of Moses, i. e. as *inspired*, unless they had been constrained by the most cogent proofs to acknowledge their divine authority? No. They would have treated them in the same scornful and contumelious manner as the infatuated Jehoiakim, sitting in his winter-house, with the fire burning on the hearth, treated the Prophetic Roll of Jeremiah [4]; they would have cut them into shreds, and destroyed them. But no: they did not dare to do so. They received them; they bowed their heads before them with reverential awe, and acknowledged them to be the oracles of God.

Thus even the sins of the Jews have been made instrumental in proving the Inspiration of the Old Testament. Their sins by which they broke the commands contained in the Old Testament, show that, if they had been able, they would have rejected those Books by which their sins are condemned. But they received them as divine. They carry them every where in their hands. Even to this day they wander about, a national

[3] Isa. lviii. 1.   [4] Jer. xxxvi. 22.

Cain, of nearly twenty centuries, having killed their own brother Abel—the true Shepherd of the sheep, Christ Jesus,—and bear about with them the mark of God [5].

8. Here also we have another proof that *no alteration* has ever been made in the Old Testament. The Prophets of God rebuke the People for their sins. But the Prophetical Books do not contain a single syllable of reproof addressed to the Jewish People for the sin of altering their Scriptures. *If* the People had ever committed so heinous a sin as that, it must have been noticed by the Prophets. And since those books do not give any hint that such alteration was ever attempted, we may rest assured, that the Hebrew Scriptures were preserved inviolate by the Hebrew People.

VI. Let us now fix our eyes on the historical epoch when those Scriptures were completed. This was after the return of the Jews from Babylon; in the time of Ezra, about 440 years before Christ.

Almighty God then raised up holy men, who revised the copies of the Old Testament, and were commissioned to add some writings to them, and to seal up the Scriptures, and to deliver them to future ages. Ezra himself, *the Priest of God and Scribe* [6], was one of these; and with him were the prophets Haggai, Zechariah, and Malachi, whose

[5] Gen. iv. 15.   [6] Ezra vii. 6. 10. 12.

The external evidence of the Inspiration of the Old Testament is confirmed by internal.

divine mission has been proved by the fulfilment of their Prophecies. The sacred Volume was then closed [7]. Malachi is called by the Jews "the Seal of the Prophets." The voice of Prophecy ceased with him, and it remained silent for four hundred years, when it sounded forth again at the Coming of Christ.

VII. The pious Israelite, who meditated on these facts, would see strong reason to remain stedfast in the belief of his forefathers, that the Books of the Old Testament were given by *Inspiration of God*. And the more he examined the contents of those Scriptures, the more he would be convinced that this belief is true. The beauty,

---

[7] See *Josephus* c. Apion. i. § 8, and the assertions of the Hebrew Rabbis in the *Mishna*, tom. iv. p. 409, ed. Surenhusii, Amst. 1702, and *Buxtorfii* Tiberias, capp. x. and xi. pp. 90—99, ed. Basil, 1665. *Prideaux's* Connexion, part i. books v. vi. *Bp. Beveridge* on the VIth Article, p. 271, ed. Oxf. 1840, and *Hävernick*, Einleitung, § 8, pp. 27—38, and *Dr. W. Lee* on Inspiration, p. 302.

Ezra, Haggai, Zechariah, and Malachi *revised* the copies, and closed the Canon of the Old Testament. But the notion that Ezra *restored* the Old Testament, after it had been destroyed, is an apocryphal fable. Some ancient Christian Fathers are cited in support of it. *Irenæus* iii. 21. Cp. *Euseb.* H. E. v. 8. *Clemens Alex.* Strom. 1. xxii. *Tertullian* de Cultu Mulier. c. 3. *S. Jerome* c. Helvid. c. 3. But they do not maintain it. The work De Mirab. Script. (ii. 33) ascribed to S. Augustine, and quoted by some as countenancing that fable, is spurious. The Christian Fathers bear testimony to the genuine Jewish tradition that Ezra and the Prophets with him revised and completed the Canon of the Old Testament.

majesty, and simplicity of the Hebrew Scriptures; their adaptation to the nature and needs of mankind; the holiness of their precepts, the harmony of all their parts, extending through a thousand years, the fulfilment of their prophecies, the blessings conferred on those who received and obeyed them, would establish him more firmly in that faith.

This faith of the ancient people of God is our faith also: we receive the Old Testament from the hands of those, to whom, as the Apostle says, *were committed the oracles of God.*

VIII. A few words may be said here, in reply to a sceptical objection.

"You say that you receive Moses, David, and Isaiah, on the testimony of the Jews; but did not the Jews reject Jesus Christ? What rational ground," we are asked, " can you assign for disregarding the decision of the Jews in the case of Jesus, and accepting it submissively in the case of Moses, David, and Isaiah [8] ?"

To this question it may be replied, that the pious and devout Jews, who received Moses, David, and Isaiah, did *not reject* Jesus Christ. Nay rather, *because* they received the Prophets, *therefore* they *received* Jesus Christ. Their language was, *We have found Him of Whom Moses*

---

[8] These words are transcribed from a Volume recently published by a sceptical writer.

and the Prophets did write, Jesus of Nazareth the son of Joseph[9].

True it is, that some Jews who held the Old Testament in their hands, but did not *understand the voices of the Prophets, which were read in their synagogues every Sabbath day, fulfilled them in condemning Him*[1], and thus, even by their unbelief, they proved the Truth and Inspiration of those Prophets. For, those *Prophets had foretold*, that many of the Jews, to whom the Prophecies concerning Christ were delivered, would *not* understand and believe them. For example, Isaiah asks, when prophesying of Christ, *Lord, who hath believed our report*[2]? He *anticipates unbelief.* Wonderful indeed it was, that the unbelieving Jews fulfilled those Prophecies, by doing those very things to Jesus Christ which those Prophecies foretold that they would do[3]. Thus the Unbelief of those who *fulfilled* those Prophecies by rejecting Christ, is an argument for the truth of those Prophecies, and for the wisdom of those who *understood* them and *received* Him. Their unbelief strengthens our belief.

Indeed, here is another evidence of God's Divine power in preserving the Scriptures, and of Christ's truth, concerning whom those Scrip-

---

[9] John i. 45.   [1] Acts xiii. 27.

[2] Isa. liii. 1. See St. John's comment on that passage of Isaiah, John xii. 38—40. See also the prophecies on the *blindness* of the Jews, Ps. lxix. 24. Isa. vi. 9. Cp. Acts xxviii. 26.

[3] Acts xiii. 27.

tures speak. We Christians receive Jesus Christ on the evidence of those Prophecies which are guarded by Jews who reject Christ. Therefore it cannot be alleged by the adversaries of Christianity, that we have tampered with the documents by which we prove its truth. Those documents come to us through the Jews. We appeal to the Old Testament, which has been preserved by them who hate us. The Jews in their dispersion carry about with them and guard carefully the Title-deeds of Christ Whom they have crucified. From the words of Moses, David, and Isaiah, in their hands, we prove the Divine mission of Jesus Christ [4].

IX. Let us now review what has been said. As soon as the *Pentateuch* was written, God provided for its safe custody. He enshrined it in the Holy of Holies, and placed it under the wings of the Cherubim. Thus God Himself declared it to be divine. That Book was a precious jewel set in a holy casket by His hand. Copies were to be made of it. Kings were to write them. "The Holy Spirit spake *by the Prophets*," and added their writings to the Law of Moses. The divine Institution of the weekly Sabbath, and of the

[4] This argument is eloquently urged by *S. Justin Martyr*, Cohortat. ad Græcos, cap. 13, and by *S. Augustine* in Psalm xl. and lvi. Proferimus codices ab inimicis ut confundamus alios inimicos. Codicem portat Judæus, unde credat Christianus. Librarii nostri facti sunt Judæi. See also his treatise c. Faustum, xii. c. 13, and De Unitate Ecclesiæ, c. 16.

yearly National Festivals, promoted the study of the Law, and bare witness to its truth. The dispersion of the Levites as the Expositors of the Law, throughout the Holy Land, and the raising up of Prophets, who were God's Messengers, were providential arrangements for preserving the Old Testament, and for assuring the People of its divine authority. The national calamities of the Hebrew People were made subservient to the same end. The dissolution of the Twelve Tribes into two separate kingdoms, and the downfall of those Kingdoms, and the dispersion of the Ten Tribes and of the Two Tribes into all parts of the world, where Synagogues were built for the reading of the Scriptures on the Sabbath days, and the universal consent of all those scattered Tribes, receiving the same Bible and venerating it as the Word of God, have also been instrumental in guarding and diffusing the Old Testament, and in guaranteeing its integrity and truth.

These divine dispensations are clear evidences of design. They are witnesses of a providential superintendence, watching over the Old Testament for fifteen hundred years from the days of Moses to those of Christ. Almighty God speaks by them, and proclaims the Integrity, the Truth, and Inspiration of the Old Testament.

This testimony extends to the *whole* of the Old Testament. It covers the entire Volume.

That providential care has been also continued from the age of Christ to this hour,—that is, for near two thousand years. Even the rejection of Christ by the Jews, and their hostility to Christianity, have been made ministerial to the safe custody of the Scriptures, and to the proof of their Truth and Inspiration.

The care with which God has guarded the Books of the Old Testament has not been relaxed for a moment since they were written. He that watcheth over them *neither slumbers nor sleeps* [5]. Nay rather, that providential care has manifested itself more clearly in every successive age.

The Pentateuch, as soon as it was written, was placed in the Holy of Holies, and was enshrined under the wings of the Cherubim.

X. But we, who are *Christians*, do not stop here. We have far stronger evidences of the genuineness, veracity, and inspiration of the Books of the Old Testament than were ever vouchsafed to the *Jews*. The *whole* of the OLD TESTAMENT has been placed under the protection of the INCARNATE WORD. It is safe under the guardianship of JESUS CHRIST, *Who is the same yesterday, and to-day, and for ever* [6].

This will be proved, with God's help, in the following lecture.

[5] Ps. cxxi. 4.   [6] Heb. xiii. 8.

LECTURE III.

Luke iv. 14—17.

And Jesus returned in the power of the Spirit into Galilee: and there went out a fame of Him through all the region round about.

And He taught in their synagogues, being glorified of all.

And He came to Nazareth, where He had been brought up: and as His custom was, He went into the Synagogue on the Sabbath day, and stood up for to read. And there was delivered unto Him the Book of the Prophet Esaias.

On what grounds do we receive the whole of the Old Testament as the Inspired Word of God?

I. To this question an answer has been already given;—We receive the whole of the Old Testament as such, on the authority of God Himself speaking in the universal consent and practice of His own People, the Jews, to whom, as St. Paul says, *were committed the oracles of God*[1], that is to say, who were *entrusted* with the guardianship of the Books of the Old Testament.

II. But this is not all. We must now ascend to a still higher point than this. We must proceed to show, that this testimony to the Inspiration of

[1] Rom. iii. 1.

the Old Testament is confirmed and verified by the infallible witness of our Lord and Saviour JESUS CHRIST. The INCARNATE WORD Himself sets His own divine seal on the Written Word. The Son of God delivers to us all the Books of the Old Testament as the inspired Oracles of God. He in whom dwelleth *all the fulness of the Godhead*, He who is the *Power of God*, and *the Wisdom of God*, He in whom are all the *treasures of wisdom and knowledge*, He who is the *Light of the World*, He who is *the Way, the Truth, and the Life*, He *Who is God*, and *by Whom all things were made* [2], proclaims the *truth* and *inspiration* of the Old Testament.

How, it may be asked, is this proposition proved?

How can it be shown, that we can appeal to the testimony of the SON of GOD in support of our belief in the Truth and Inspiration of the Old Testament?

III. To answer this question, we must first show the *historical truth* of the *New* Testament.

Let us, then, *begin* with taking into our hands the *Four Gospels*, which profess to relate the sayings, actions and sufferings of Jesus Christ.

1. We can prove by *external* testimony, that these *Four Gospels* existed, in the same state as that in which they now exist, at the end of the first century of the Christian era, that is, nearly

---

[2] Col. ii. 9. 1 Cor. i. 24. Col. ii. 3. John viii. 12. John xiv. 6. John i. 1—3.

Proof of the truth of the Gospels, and consequently, of Christ's divine authority.

1800 years ago. Ancient authors testify, that St. John's Gospel was written at that time, and that he acknowledged the truth of the other three Gospels,—those of St. Matthew, St. Mark, and St. Luke,—and added his own Gospel, to complete the Evangelical History³.

2. We can prove by *external* evidence, that those Gospels, completed by St. John, were received, and were publicly read ' as *true* histories by large communities of men, who had the best opportunities of testing and knowing their truth; namely, by the Christians, and by the Christian Churches which existed in primitive times. They would not have read those Gospels in their public worship, unless they had believed them; and they would not have believed them unless they were true.

We can show that those persons and Churches could not have been deceived as to the credibility of those Gospels. And they could not have deceived others. They were plain men. Their adversaries reproached them as having no learning, wealth, or power. We can show that they had

---

³ See *Clemens Alexandrin.* ap. Euseb. vi. 15; cp. *Euseb.* iii. 24. *Canon Muratorian.* in Routh's Reliquiæ Sacræ, iv. p. 2. *Victorin.* in Apocalyps. Bibl. Patr. Max. iii. 41. *Theodor. Mopsuest.* in Catenâ ad Joann. in Dr. Mill's Greek Test. p. 198.

S. *Irenæus* iii. 1; iii. 11. 7—9. See *S. Justin Martyr,* Apol. i. 67. Cp. *Westcott* on the Canon of the New Test., p. 365 and p. 367: "No one at present will deny that they (the Gospels, &c.) occupied the same position in the estimation of Christians in the time of Irenæus (i. e. in the second century) as they hold now."

no earthly interest to serve in asserting the truth of those Gospels. On the contrary, the assertion of that truth exposed them to the loss of all worldly things. They resisted all earthly temptations, they endured, cheerfully endured, all privations, sufferings, and torments for its sake [5]; they were stoned, beheaded, crucified, burnt, cast to the wild beasts, as heathen historians testify; these things, and more, they suffered in defence of the Truth of the Four Gospels.

3. Now mark the result.

That self-same Power, the Power of Heathen, Imperial Rome, which at first persecuted the Christians, and beheaded the Christians, and crucified the Christians, and cast the Christians to wild beasts for asserting the truth of the Gospels; *that* very Power, that Roman Power, that Heathen Power, that Imperial Power, that Power

---

[5] Especially in the persecution under the Roman Emperor Diocletian, A.D. 303, who endeavoured to destroy the copies of the Christian Scriptures, and burnt many of those writings. See *Euseb*. Hist. Eccl. viii. 2. *Lactant*. de Mort. Persecutor. c. xii. The Christians who were tempted by fear to surrender copies of them to their heathen persecutors were called "traditores" by their brethren. See the Passio of S. Felix in *Baluzii* Miscellanea ii. p. 77.—*Gieseler*, Church Hist. § 55 and 56. *Routh*, Reliquiæ Sacræ, tom. v. p. 341. " The holy Martyrs in their Acts (collected by *Ruinart*, Amst. 1713, see pp. 87. 89. 356, 357. 394) proclaim in the presence of their Judges, that the Holy Books received by the Christians at that time,—the Gospels and the other Books,—are revered by them, and are believed to be directly inspired, and are affectionately guarded by them unto death, and are not to be given up to any one."

which then ruled the world, was at length convinced of the *Truth of the Four Gospels*, which were received as God's Word by the Christians. That self-same Roman Power, the Queen and Mistress of the World, was converted to the cause of the Gospels. She publicly owned her conversion; she acknowledged that those whom she had put to death as Christians, were Martyrs to the Truth. She revered the memories of Peter and Paul whom she had killed. She, who by the force of arms had made the Nations of the world to pass under her military yoke, humbly and meekly bowed her own head beneath the mild yoke of Christ. She changed her Heathen Temples into Christian Churches. And in those Heathen Temples, when changed into Christian Churches, the Four Gospels of Matthew and Mark, Luke and John were thenceforth read as *true* and *divine histories*. She placed those Four Gospels upon Thrones in her own Council Chambers [6]; and the Cross of Jesus of Nazareth, who had been crucified by the Roman Governor Pontius Pilate,—yes, the Cross of Jesus of Nazareth, of obscure Nazareth in despised Galilee,—dislodged the Roman Eagle from the military standards of the Roman Legions, and was set on

---

[6] The Emperor Constantine thus speaks in his oration to the Bishops at Nicæa: "The Gospels and the Apostolic writings and the oracles of the ancient Prophets clearly teach us what to believe of God. Let us receive the solution of the question before us from the *divinely inspired words* (ἐκ τῶν θεοπνεύστων λόγων)." *Theodoret*, 1. 5.

the Imperial Diadem of the Roman Masters of the world.

These are facts as clear as the noonday sun. And in the face of these facts, who can say that the Four Gospels are not historically *true*?

4. This proposition then being admitted, that the Gospels are *true*, it follows, that there is such a Person as Jesus Christ; and that He did indeed perform those wonderful works, which He is related in the Four Gospels to have done; that in the presence of multitudes,—many of them His bitter enemies,—He healed the sick, cast out devils, raised the dead; that He knew the thoughts and searched the hearts of men, and foretold future events; that He rose again from the dead, and ascended into heaven: in a word, that He displayed power, knowledge, and wisdom infinitely greater than were ever shown by any of the children of men; and that He *was* indeed, what He *claimed* to be, and what by His mighty and merciful works He *proved* Himself to be,—the *Son of the Living God*, the *Light of the World*, the *Creator and Lord of all*, coequal, coeternal with the Father[7].

5. This point being proved, let us bear in mind,—as is evident from *external* testimony,—that the Old Testament existed in our Lord's age, in the same condition as that in which it exists now. This has been already shewn in the last lecture.

[7] John viii. 12. 58; x. 30.

Jesus Christ acknowledged all the Old Testament to be given by Inspiration of God.

The Jewish Nation of that age received *the whole* of the Old Testament, not as the word of man, but as the Word of God. They guarded the sacred Text of the Old Testament with scrupulous fidelity and unremitting vigilance; they read the Old Testament publicly, Sabbath after Sabbath, throughout the year, in their Synagogues, in almost all countries of the world; and, by reason of the multiplication of copies of the Original and of Translations, that were requisite for this general public reading of the Old Testament in every clime, it was not possible for any one to tamper with the Text of the Old Testament, or to make any change in it, either by interpolation or mutilation.

6. Such was the state of things before Christ's Coming, and at His Coming into the world. And ever since that time, the Text of the Old Testament has been guarded by the twofold, independent, antagonistic custody of the Jewish Synagogue and of the Christian Church; so that we may confidently say, that the Old Testament which is now read in the Churches of England is the same as the Old Testament which was read in the Jewish Synagogues of our Lord's age. The Old Testament in *our* hands is the same as the Old Testament which was in the hands of JESUS CHRIST.

7. Contemplate therefore JESUS CHRIST holding in His hands the Old Testament. How did He treat it? He, Who proved by His wonderful

deeds and words that He was wiser than all the children of men, He Who is our Divine Teacher, the *True Light which lighteth every man* [8], He in Whom dwelleth all *the fulness of the Godhead,* He in Whom are hid all *treasures of wisdom and knowledge* [9], He Who came into the world to *bear witness unto the truth,* how did He treat the Old Testament? Did He treat it as "a common book?" Did He say that *some* parts of it are *inspired,* and that *other* parts are *not inspired?* Did He say that *some* portions of it are *genuine,* and that *other* portions are *forged?* Did He say that *some* of its contents are *true,* and that *others* are *false?*

The answer to these questions is easy. The Jews guarded the Books of the Old Testament. They read those Books in their Synagogues every Sabbath, and they venerated all those Books,—they revered *every part* of those Books,—as true, as genuine, and as given by the inspiration of God. To quote the words of their own writer, Josephus[1], it was "a principle innate in every Jew to regard those Books as oracles of God, and to cleave to them, yea, and to die gladly for them."

Now, how did our Blessed Lord treat this their national belief in the Inspiration of the Old Testament?

Did Christ *censure* the Jews for ascribing the

---

[8] John i. 9; xix. 37.   [9] Col. ii. 3. 9.
[1] See above, pp. 36, 37.

Old Testament to God? Did He *blame* them for accepting *every part of it* as God's Word? *If* the Old Testament is merely the word of man, or *if any portion* of it is false, *if* any part of it is a forgery, Christ would have *reproved* those who attributed *the whole* of it to God. He, Who was so zealous for His Father's honour that He drove the buyers and sellers even from the outer courts of His Father's House [2], would have rebuked those who ascribed the erring words of sinful man to the God of all Wisdom, Holiness, and Truth. He would not have made Himself an accomplice with those who put forth counterfeit coin in the Name of the King of kings. He would not have abetted those who stamped that adulterated coinage with the Divine image and superscription, and circulated it throughout the world. The Son of God would have resented such an ascription; He would have denounced such an imputation, as a profane outrage and insult against the awful majesty of God.

But hear what the Gospels relate of Christ.

Take, for instance, the chapter to which we have referred at the beginning of this lecture—the fourth chapter of St. Luke's Gospel. It begins with the history of the Temptation. There our Lord defeats the Tempter with the *sword of the Spirit, which is the Word of God* [3]. Thrice Satan assailed Him, and thrice Christ foiled him with this

---

[2] Matt. xxi. 10. Mark xi. 15. . Luke xix. 45. John ii. 15.
[3] Eph. vi. 14.

weapon, "*It is written*[4]." It is remarkable that the Son of God vanquished Satan by three verses of the *Pentateuch, that* very part of Scripture which is now disparaged by some among us who profess themselves Masters of Israel. Would Christ have used the Pentateuch in such a conflict as that, and would Satan have fled before Him, if that weapon had not been divine?

But further, our Lord worked miracles; and preached in the Synagogues of Galilee. He came to Nazareth. *As His custom was, He went into the Synagogue on the Sabbath Day. He there stood up to read.* In those Synagogues the Books of the Old Testament were *delivered to Him* as *the oracles of God,* and He received them as such. "To-day," He said, " is *this Scripture* fulfilled in your ears." On another occasion He said, *It is easier for heaven and earth to pass than one tittle of the Law to fail*[5]. Who then will venture to say that the Pentateuch is blemished with error? And again, He declared that *the Scripture cannot be broken*[6], and that not *a jot or tittle of the Law would pass away till all was fulfilled.* Who then will assert that it is weak and fragile? The Son of God, when on earth, communicated with the Jews, Sabbath after Sabbath, in public worship; He *took part with them* in reading and expounding the Scriptures of the Old Testament *as the inspired Word of God.* Thus He declared

---

[4] Luke iv. 4. 8. 12.   [5] Luke xvi. 17. Cp. Matt. v. 18.
[6] λυθῆναι, John x. 35. Matt. x. 18.

that their belief in its Inspiration is true. He required all to receive it.

8. To give, if possible, greater solemnity to this declaration, Christ put it into the mouth of the Father of the faithful, Abraham, the Representative of all true Israelites; He uttered it by the voice of Abraham, removed from this world, and dwelling in the blessed society of the spirits of the departed, of Moses, and David, and Isaiah, and all the Prophets. In the parable of Lazarus and the Rich Man, in which our Lord uplifts the veil which separates this world from the world of spirits, Christ reveals to us Abraham, and He makes Abraham speak that remarkable speech, *They have Moses and the Prophets,* let them hear them. *If they hear not Moses and the Prophets, neither will they be persuaded though one rose from the dead*[7]. Awfully solemn words, uttered by the Lord of Life, speaking by Abraham, the *friend of God. They have Moses and the Prophets.* Who therefore of us, that entertains a blessed hope that his own spirit may be carried by Angels at his own death into *Abraham's bosom,* and be there in peace with those who have departed in the true faith and fear of God, will venture to deny that the Books which the Jews regarded as the Books of Moses and the Prophets, are not what they believed them to be,—*true, genuine, and divine?*

9. Yet more, after that the Son of God Himself

[7] Luke xvi. 29. 31.

had overcome Death, and when, on the evening of His glorious Resurrection, He walked with the two disciples to Emmaus, and when, on that same evening, He appeared to His Apostles, He appealed to the Books of the Old Testament as true, and as inspired by God; *Beginning at Moses and all the Prophets, He expounded to them in all the Scriptures the things concerning Himself*[8]*;* and He said, *These are the words which I spake unto you, that all things must be fulfilled which were written in the Law of Moses, and in the Prophets, and in the Psalms, concerning Me*[9].

Thus then our Lord and Saviour Jesus Christ, who is "God of God, Light of Light, Very God of Very God," has pronounced His divine verdict in behalf of the Truth, the Integrity, and Inspiration of the Old Testament. And this divine verdict, let us observe, applies to *every part of the Old Testament.* It covers the whole; it applies to every portion of all those Books which the Jews received as Holy Scripture.

Therefore we may sum up by saying, that the SON of GOD delivers to us the whole of the Old Testament, and commands us to receive the whole as the Word of the Living God.

10. This argument from Christ's acceptance of the Old Testament is so strong, that they who disparage the Old Testament have strained every nerve to weaken it. They allege that Christ

---

[8] Luke xxiv. 27. [9] Luke xxiv. 44.

spoke only as a "*learned Jewish Rabbi*[1]," or, that He "*accommodated Himself*" to the popular belief of the Jews, and did not declare *His own opinions* concerning the Old Testament.

Surely the weakness of such allegations as these, and (must we not say?) their impiety, leads us to recognize more clearly the force of the argument from Christ's reception of the Old Testament.

Did Jesus Christ speak only as a "learned Rabbi?" Did any learned Rabbi ever say, as Christ did, "*I am the Way, the Truth, and the Life*[2]," "*I and My Father are One*[3]?" Did any learned Rabbi ever say, "*Before Abraham was, I am*[4]," and, "*For this cause came I into the world to bear witness unto the truth; every one that is of the truth heareth My Voice*[5]?" Did any learned Rabbi ever say, "*I am the Light of the world?*[6]" Did any learned Rabbi ever say, "*Heaven and earth shall pass away, but My words shall not pass away*[7]?" Did any learned Rabbi ever say, "*I am Alpha and Omega, the Beginning and the Ending, the First and the Last, the Almighty*[8]?" And as for *accommodating* Himself, as it is alleged, to popular errors of the Jews, what a monstrous proposition is that! Strange accommodation

---

[1] *Bishop Colenso* on the Pentateuch, Pt. i. p. xxxi. Pt. ii. p. xvii. *Davidson's* Introduction to the Old Testament, vol. i. p. 127.
[2] John xiv. 6.   [3] John x. 30.   [4] John viii. 58.
[5] John xviii. 37.   [6] John viii. 12.   [7] Mark xiii. 31.
[8] Rev. i. 8.

indeed! Did not Jesus Christ *denounce eight woes against the Jews for their sins*[9]? and did they not cry "*Crucify Him, crucify Him*"[1] because He would *not accommodate* Himself to their popular notions of a temporal and triumphant Messiah?

Therefore we may confidently appeal to the testimony of the SON of GOD, coequal and coeternal with the Father, as avouching the Truth and Divine Inspiration of the Old Testament.

11. Nor is this all. Christ promised that after His ascension He would send the Divine Comforter, God the HOLY GHOST, to *teach* His Apostles *all things; to guide them into all truth*, to *dwell with them* and to be *in them*[2].

The Holy Apostles, being taught by the Holy Spirit whom Christ sent down from heaven, declared that the Old Testament is inspired by God. Thus St. Peter speaks not only the opinion of his own Nation, but utters the judgment of the HOLY SPIRIT, when he says of the Hebrew Prophets, that *Prophecy came not by the will of man*, but that they spake what they *spake, being borne along by the Holy Ghost*[3]; and St. Paul says that he *believes all things which are written in the Law and the Prophets*[4], and he reminds Timothy that the Scriptures which he had known from his child-

---

[9] See Matt. xxiii. 13—39.
[2] John xiv. 26; xvi. 7. 13; xiv. 16, 17.
[4] Acts xxiv. 14.
[1] Luke xxiii. 21.
[3] 2 Pet. i. 21.

hood are *holy*, and are *the things which are able*[5] to make him wise unto salvation through faith that is in Christ Jesus; and he adds, that *every Scripture*—that is, every part of Scripture—*is given by inspiration of God*, or as the words signify, is *filled with the breath of God*[6].

This Apostolic testimony to the truth and inspiration of the Old Testament is the testimony of GOD the HOLY GHOST, who came from heaven to *teach the Apostles all things*, and to *guide them into all truth*.

IV. Let us now apply these things to ourselves and to the circumstances of our own times.

1. Is the Old Testament *true*? Is it *from heaven*? Is it *all true*? Is it *all inspired*? These questions are now current among us. Books are put into our hands, written, it would seem, by shrewd men, distinguished by literary attainments, and by philosophic calmness and research, who appear to have inquired with candour and impartiality into the evidences of the Truth and Inspiration of the Old Testament, and *not* to have been convinced that it is of divine origin. We hear it alleged by some, that it can

[5] τὰ δυνάμενα, "*the* things that are able." 2 Tim. iii. 15. Observe the definite Article.

[6] The testimonies of the Ancient Fathers of the Church in succession after the Apostles, witnessing to the Inspiration of the Old Testament, as well as the New, may be seen collected by *Dr. Routh*, Reliquiæ Sacræ, vol. v. pp. 336—353, and by the *Rev. Canon Westcott*, Introduction to the Study of the Gospels, pp. 383—418.

be shown from investigations of Geologists, that the physical phenomena of the Earth are inconsistent with the record of Creation in the Book of Genesis. We hear it argued by others, who seem to be proficients in the study of Morals and Metaphysics, that to believe all mankind to have been involved in guilt by the sin of Adam and Eve, is not consistent with the reverence due to the Justice and Benevolence of God: and that it is derogatory to His Wisdom and Foresight, to suppose that He should have destroyed His own work of Creation by the general devastation of the Flood.

What, again, they ask, are we to say of such strange and incredible narratives as those which are found in the Old Testament, such as the *standing still of the sun* at the command of Joshua, or concerning the speaking of *Balaam's ass*, and the coming forth of the Prophet *Jonah* from the whale's belly after three days? What are we to think of these things?

Again, it is said by some persons of high reputation among us, reviving the sceptical objections of Porphyry[7] which were exploded by S. Jerome[8] fourteen hundred years ago, that the prophecies of *Daniel*[9] bear marks of having been

---

[7] And of some Jews *since our Lord's age*, who perceive that the Messiah must be already come, if Daniel is a Prophet. See *Hottinger,* Thesaur. Philol. p. 504.

[8] See *S. Jerome*, Præfat. in Danielem, tom. iii. p. 1071, ed. Benedict. Paris, 1704.

[9] "Essays and Reviews," pp. 69. 76.

composed *after* the events which they profess to foretell,—and, in fact, are no prophecies at all.

2. To those who may make these, and all such allegations as these, impugning the Truth, Genuineness, or Inspiration of the Old Testament, we would put this question,—

Whom shall we believe,—you, or JESUS CHRIST?

You allege, that there are certain things in the Old Testament which you cannot reconcile with results of your physical researches, or with your moral and metaphysical theories; and you therefore reject the Old Testament, and require us to surrender it in deference to your authority.

But in this great question—in this most momentous question of eternal life or eternal death — we ask again, *Whom* shall we believe, *whom* shall we follow? You, or JESUS CHRIST? Shall we imagine that you, the creatures of a day, have a clearer insight into the Laws of Nature, than He who made the worlds[1], and who controlled the Laws of Nature by a word? Shall we suppose that you have more knowledge of the history and structure of the Universe, than He who swayed the Elements, and walked on the Sea, and calmed the Storm, and made the Earth give up her dead, and mounted on the clouds of Heaven? Shall we listen to those metaphysical theorists, who would have us give up the Old Testament, which was received as a Divine Book by Him who read the heart, and knew what was in man, and foretold

[1] John i. 3. Heb. i. 2.

things to come? Shall we give credence to those Moralists, who reject the Old Testament, which was acknowledged to be God's Word by that Divine Teacher of Moral Virtue who preached the Sermon on the Mount; and whose Religion, wherever it has been received, has emancipated the Slave, and beautified Marriage, and has given a grace and dignity to Woman, which she never before possessed since she was Eve in Paradise, and has opened a pure well-spring of blessing and of joy in every Christian family, and prepares its members, by the discipline of love on earth, for the life of angels in heaven?

In what appertains to the Word of God let us not pretend to be wiser than the Son of God. Let us not reject a single iota of the Old Testament, with frail and fallible children of men, but reverently receive the whole with the Son of God.

He has delivered to us the Old Testament: He who is now enthroned in glory commands us to receive it. Alas! for those who *refuse Him that speaketh from heaven*[2]. For He has warned us that he that *believeth and is baptized shall be saved, and he that believeth not shall be damned*[3]. Inexpressibly awful words, uttered by the Judge of all, who *hath the Keys of Hell and Death*[4]. He will one day *be revealed in flaming fire taking vengeance on them that obey not the Gospel*[5]. And then it will be seen by all, and it will be felt by

---

[2] Heb. xii. 25.   [3] Mark xvi. 16.
[4] Rev. i. 18.   [5] 2 Thess. i. 7, 8.

the children of darkness, that while He is infinite in mercy to all who believe and obey Him, yet to all who do not believe Him, *our God is a consuming fire*[6].

3. Looking, then, to Christ holding the Old Testament in his hands, we are not staggered by any difficulties in it. We *expect* to find difficulties in a Revelation from a Being like God to such a creature as man. We even rejoice in these difficulties. We do not fear them as enemies, but welcome them as allies, and embrace them as friends; for they are occasions of our growth in grace. They exercise our humility. They are the leaves and flowers of which our heavenly crown is woven. They remind us of our own weakness and ignorance, and of the power and wisdom of Christ. They send us to Him, and to the Gospel. They make us to go and sit down as little children at the feet of Jesus Christ.

If we may so speak, before the Coming of Christ into the world, there were many clouds and mists which veiled the true sense of Scripture from the sight. But many of those clouds and mists have been now dispelled by the Gospel; and the time is coming when they will all be dispersed by the glorious beams of the Sun of Righteousness, Jesus Christ.

4. Take, for instance, the *standing still of the sun* at the command of Joshua. I have elsewhere examined in detail the objections to this state-

[6] Heb. xii. 29.

ment⁷. Let us remember that Joshua was a type and figure of Jesus Christ. All his doings have some reference to his great Antitype. "There is scarcely an action of Joshua (says Bp. Pearson), which is not clearly predictive of our Saviour." That great miracle will hereafter be seen to have a prophetic relation to Christ. This will be manifest at the Great Day, when our Jesus comes with His Armies of Angels to subdue His enemies, and to settle His faithful soldiers and servants in the heavenly Canaan. The Sun will then stand still, the Moon will be stayed, the whole system of the visible Universe will not be dissolved, till Christ's Victory is complete. *He must reign till He hath put all enemies under His feet. And when all things shall be subdued unto Him,—then the heavens will pass away with a great noise, and the elements will melt with fervent heat, the earth also and the works that are therein shall be burnt up.* Then there will be a great *sunset.* Then His Mediatorial Kingdom, which He has as *Jesus* or *Joshua,* will be finished, then will the *end be, when He shall have put down all rule and all authority and power: and God will be all in all*⁸.

5. Thus again, as to the *history of Balaam.* It may be a difficulty to some. But it will remind every Christian reader, that the Apostle of Christ, St. Peter, who was enabled by Christ to

---

⁷ See the notes in my Commentary on Joshua x.
⁸ 1 Cor. xv. 24—28.

heal the sick, and raise the dead, and to speak with tongues [9], and to discern the spirits, as in the case of Ananias [1], and to foretell the future, has referred to the history of Balaam in the second chapter of his second Epistle. The Holy Spirit speaking by St. Peter accepts the history of Balaam, and explains its inner meaning, and reminds us how by that signal example, *the Lord, who opened the mouth of the ass,* showed, that even the most despised of the brute creatures are wiser and more clear-sighted than a disobedient Prophet, or a sceptical Philosopher. *The dumb ass speaking with man's voice, forbad the madness of the Prophet* [2].

6. Thus also as to the *history of Jonah in the whale's belly.* It may be a difficulty with some; but in reading that history every Christian student will recollect, that Jesus Christ has adopted and authenticated that history, and has applied and appropriated it to Himself. *As Jonas was three days and three nights in the whale's belly, so* (said Christ) *shall the Son of Man be three days and three nights in the heart of the earth* [3]. The Christian reader will observe, that Christ's reference to the history of Jonah is interwoven with Christ's prophecy concerning Himself; and he will remember that Christ's word was proved to be true by the fulfilment of that prophecy.

---

[9] Acts ii. 4; iii. 7; ix. 34. 40. [1] Acts v. 3.
[2] 2 Pet. ii. 16. May I refer to my notes on Num. xxii. ?
[3] Matt. xii. 40. May I also refer to my notes on Jonah i. ?

Christ *was* three days and three nights in the heart of the earth; and He then raised Himself. Thus Christ's authorization of Jonah's history is verified by the fulfilment of Christ's prophecy concerning Himself, of Whom Jonah was a type. Let us not read the history of Jonah by the feeble glimmerings of a purblind sciolism, but by the clear light of Christ's glorious Gospel, and we shall see the proof of its truth in His Burial and Resurrection. Thus these Scriptural difficulties will be dissolved by a spiritual alchymy in the crucible of faith.

7. Once more: the unbeliever alleges that the prophecies of *Daniel* correspond so minutely with the events that they profess to predict that they must be posterior to those events. A strange allegation! As if there were any past or future with God! As if He, who spake by the Prophets, does not see all things present at once! It is enough for us to know that the Book of Daniel, as it is in our hands now, was in the hands of the Jewish nation of our Lord's age; and was received by them as inspired [4]; and that what they received as inspired was also received as such by Jesus Christ. Indeed He expressly owns Daniel as a prophet. "When ye shall see the abomina-

---

[4] See the remarkable testimony of the Jewish historian *Josephus*, Antiquities, book x. chapters 10—12. See also *Maimonides*, More Nevochim, ii. 45, who says "*Daniel*, the Psalms, &c., are all written by the *Holy Spirit*." May I be allowed to refer here to my *Introduction and Notes* to the Book of Daniel?

Christians enjoy greater advantages than the Hebrews, even with regard to the Hebrew Scriptures.

tion of desolation, spoken of by *Daniel the Prophet*[5]."—Daniel the Prophet may be no Prophet to the unbeliever; the book of Daniel may be a forgery to the sceptic of the nineteenth century; but to us, my Christian friends, let him be Daniel the Prophet; for he *was* Daniel the Prophet to his own nation, he *was* "Daniel the Prophet" to Jesus Christ.

V. Let us here acknowledge our own spiritual privileges, and our cause for thankfulness to God. The *Jews* of old were greatly favoured by Him, but how much more favoured are *we!* "What advantage hath the *Jew?*" asks the Apostle. "*Much every way*," he replies, "*chiefly because unto them were committed the oracles of God.*" And may we not much more say, "What advantage hath the *Christian?* Much every way;" even *more* than the Jew. For *we* have a stronger assurance of the Divine Inspiration of the Hebrew Scriptures than the Jews themselves had. They received the Old Testament as inspired, on the testimony of their forefathers; but it is delivered to us, as inspired, by the Son of God. Here is an inexpressible comfort; here indeed is a joyful assurance, in days like these, of rebuke and blasphemy. Here we have hope and peace in the sorrows of life, and in the hour of death. *Our* belief in the Truth and Inspiration of the Old

---

[5] Matt. xxiv. 15. Mark xiii. 14. Dan. ix. 27; xii. 11.

Testament, yes, of the *whole* of the Old Testament, rests on a foundation that can never be shaken. It rests on the testimony of Christ. Therefore we may dwell safely, and defy the storms raging around us. Let the rain descend; let the floods of Unbelief come, and the winds of false Doctrine blow, and beat upon our house; it will *not* fall, for it *is built upon a Rock* [6]. It is built upon the *Rock of Ages* [7]; it is built upon Jesus Christ. It is built on the testimony of God the Holy Ghost, whom He sent to His Apostles, to *teach them all things,* and to *guide them into all truth.*

VI. Finally, may we not say, that the written Word of God is like the INCARNATE WORD Himself,—*set for the fall, and* also *for the rising of many in Israel,* and *for a sign that shall be spoken against* [8] ?

Holy Scripture is set for our moral probation, which supposes trial and difficulty. It exhibits us to men and angels as we are. It displays what *manner of spirit we are of* [9]. It is a test and touchstone of our fitness for heaven. It proves, whether we have those moral habits and tempers of mind,—that distrust of ourselves, and that sense of our need of the light of the Holy Ghost without which no man can hope to be able to see the truth. It shows whether we possess those dispositions of meekness and docility, and

---

[6] Matt. vii. 24, 25.   [7] Isa. xxvi. 4.
[8] Luke ii. 34.   [9] Luke ix. 55.

Those difficulties will be cleared away from the eyes of those who use them aright.

readiness to weigh evidence with candour and fairness, without which no man is *fit for the kingdom of God* [1].

The *difficulties* in Scripture vanish into nothing, when they are *compared* with the evidence in *its favour;* they are merely as dust in the balance, when set against the *difficulty,* or rather the *moral impossibility,* of resisting the testimony of Jesus Christ, and of the Holy Ghost, to the truth and inspiration of the Bible. They are like mole-hills, when compared with that mountain.

Holy Scripture is set for our *fall,*—if we proudly set up our own reason against divine revelation, and in opposition to the testimony of Christ, and of the Holy Ghost, and if, with a *partial eye* to *difficulties* in *single texts* taken by themselves, and without due regard to the general scope of the whole, and to the divine evidence of its Truth and Inspiration, we take occasion to cavil at its contents, and deny its divine origin and authority. And then our cavils will be our punishment. They will be the recoil of our own sin against ourselves. They will provoke God to withdraw His grace from us, and to leave us to ourselves; and then we shall be spiritually blind. For how can we hope to see, without Him Who is the Light?

Let those who carp at Holy Scripture be earnestly and affectionately requested to consider that by so doing they oppose themselves to Christ,

[1] Luke ix. 62.

Who sets His Divine Seal upon Scripture. They rebel against Him Who is God; and Who is their future Judge, and Who will determine their sentence for ever according to their treatment of His Word. (John xii. 48.) They make Scripture, which is given to them for their joy and happiness in this world and in eternity,—to be an occasion to them of everlasting misery and shame; to be for their *fall* even into an abyss of perdition, and into the bottomless pit, and the *lake of fire*, which is the *second death*. (Rev. xx. 10, 14.)

But, on the other hand, thanks be to God, Scripture is set for our *rising*,—for our rising to heavenly glory,—if we use those difficulties aright, and are led thereby to acknowledge the weakness of our own faculties in their present state, and our consequent need of divine grace; and to exercise humility, and to thank God for what is *perfectly clear* in Holy Scripture; and to *tarry the Lord's leisure*, and to look forward with patience, faith, and hope to that blessed time, when all those difficulties will be dispersed, and the film and mist, which now cloud our spiritual vision, will be purged away; and we shall no longer see, as now, *through a glass darkly*, but shall *see face to face*, and *know even as we are known* [2].

[2] 1 Cor. xiii. 12.

LECTURE IV.

LUKE xi. 33.

No man, when he hath lighted a candle, putteth it in a secret place, neither under a bushel, but on a candlestick, that they which come in may see the light [1].

WE have been engaged in considering, what the reasons are for belief in the Inspiration of the *Old* Testament.

I. The subject now proposed for examination is;—

On what grounds do we receive the *New* Testament as the Inspired Word of God?

1. God is One, and Everlasting; and *if* the *New* Testament is from Him, we may reasonably anticipate, that the method employed by Him for assuring us of the Inspiration of the *New* Testament, will, as far as the difference of circumstances allows, be similar to that plan by which He has assured us of the Inspiration of the Old.

2. When we were asked for the reasons of our

[1] Cp. Matt. v. 15. Mark iv. 21. Luke viii. 16.

belief in the Inspiration of the *Old* Testament, our answer was,—

First, we receive the Old Testament on the authority of God Himself, speaking by the universal consent and practice of the Hebrew Nation, to which, as the Apostle says, *were committed the Oracles of God*[2].

Next we proceeded to show, that when the Son of God Himself came down from heaven, and dwelt among us, He acknowledged the truth of that belief in the Inspiration of the Old Testament. Our Blessed Lord declared His own concurrence in, and pronounced His divine approval of, this consent and practice of the Hebrew Nation, receiving all the Books of the Old Testament, as set apart from all other Volumes then existing in the world, and as holy and divine Writings, dictated by the Spirit of God.

Thirdly, when Jesus Christ had ascended into heaven, He sent the Holy Ghost to *teach* His Apostles *all things,* and to *guide them into all truth.* And they, so taught and guided, received the Old Testament as divine.

3. Our present assertion is, that Almighty God has employed similar means for assuring us of the Inspiration of the *New* Testament.

We affirm that the New Testament comes to us principally and originally from JESUS CHRIST.

---

[2] Rom. iii. 1.

We look up to heaven with the eye of Faith, and we see JESUS CHRIST, the Incarnate WORD, enthroned there in His glorious Majesty, and holding in His hands the Old and New Testaments, and delivering to us both Testaments, as the Word of the Living God.

4. In order to show the soundness of this belief, we must revert to a proposition already proved in a previous discourse, namely, that the *Four Gospels* are historically *true*[3].

That the *Four Gospels* are *true*, has been shown from the facts, that the Gospels were publicly *read* in Christian Churches in primitive times; and that they who read them could not have been deceived as to their veracity; and that they died gladly in defence of their Truth: and that eventually the Roman Empire, which at first had persecuted the Christians for belief in the Gospels, was itself converted to Christianity, and received the Gospels as *true*.

II. The *truth* of the Gospels being established, it follows that the Son of God uttered those sayings which He is related in the Gospels to have spoken.

1. Among the declarations of Christ recorded in the Gospels, we find the following: *Upon this Rock I will build My Church, and the gates of hell shall not prevail against it*[4]. *Lo, I am with you alway, even unto the end of the world*[5]. Christ

---

[3] See above, pp. 57—60.
[4] Matt. xvi. 18.   [5] Matt. xxviii. 20.

promised to send the Holy Spirit to His disciples, to *guide them into all truth*, and to *abide with them for ever. These things have I spoken unto you, being yet present with you; but the Comforter, which is the Holy Ghost, whom the Father will send in My name, He shall teach you all things, and bring all things to your remembrance, whatsoever I have said unto you* [6]. And, *When He, the Spirit of Truth, is come, He will guide you into all truth: for He shall not speak of Himself; but whatsoever He shall hear, that shall He speak, and He will show you things to come* [7]. *I will pray the Father, and He will give you another Comforter, that He may abide with you for ever, even the Spirit of Truth* [8]. And again, *I will give you a mouth and wisdom, which all your adversaries shall not be able to gainsay nor resist* [9].

The fulfilment of these promises of Christ is avouched in the history of the Acts of the Apostles [1], the truth of which is proved by its reception and public reading in the primitive Churches of Christendom.

2. Hence we may conclude, that Christ enabled His Apostles and Evangelists to reveal supernatural mysteries; and that the words which they have delivered to the Church for her perpetual instruction in divine truth, and which have been read as such in her public assemblies from their

---

[6] John xiv. 25, 26.   [7] John xvi. 13.
[8] John xiv. 16.   [9] Luke xxi. 15.
[1] Acts ii. 4.

and He instituted the Church to be a Witness of the Inspiration of the Scriptures written by them.

age until now, are *not words which man's wisdom teacheth, but which the Holy Ghost teacheth* [2].

3. Next, we may deduce from Christ's words just rehearsed, this inference—that He has instituted in the world a visible Society, called His Church, to which He has promised His perpetual presence and His Spirit, to lead it into all truth, and to abide with it unto the end.

Accordingly, we find that the Apostle St. Paul, having regard to Christ's promise of His continual presence in His Church, calls her His *Body;* and meditating on His love to His Church, and her dearness to Him, he speaks of her as united to Christ in spiritual wedlock [3]; and forasmuch as she is quickened, and taught by God the Holy Spirit dwelling in her, and publishing by her, as by a living organ, His will and word, the Apostle says, that she *is the Church of the Living God, the Pillar and Ground of the Truth* [4].

We cannot say with some persons, that we receive the Scriptures as divine merely because *we* know *who* their writers were, and that they were good men full of the Holy Ghost, and that *therefore* whatever they wrote must be inspired of God.

The truth is, we do *not* know, by *whom* some of the Books of Scripture were written [5]; and

---

[2] 1 Cor. ii. 13.   [3] Eph. v. 23—32.
[4] 1 Tim. iii. 15.
[5] E. g. the Books of Job, Judges, and others in the Old Testament. The Epistle to the Hebrews in the New Testament was, in

this uncertainty seems to have been intended to serve a providential purpose, in order that we might not attribute the authority of the Scriptures to the *men* by whose instrumentality they were written, but to *God who* wrote the Scriptures by their hands.

We receive the Books of Holy Scripture on the testimony of JESUS CHRIST, the Son of God; Who sent from heaven the Holy Ghost to *teach* His Apostles *all things* (that is, all things necessary to salvation), and to *guide them into all truth*, and to *abide for ever* in His Church; and Who testifies to the Truth and Inspiration of Holy Scripture by His Divine Witness in the Church.

III. One of the principal offices of the Church of God, ever since Scripture was written, has been to guard Scripture, and to read it openly and habitually to the people, and to authenticate it as God's Word [6].

1. We find, that as soon as the first Books of Scripture—namely, the Books of Moses—were written, they were deposited by God's command

---

all *probability*, written by St. Paul; but its *inspiration* is not only probable, but *certain:* because it is received, as inspired, by the Universal Church of God.

Besides, the *authorship* of some smaller portions of the Gospels may be matter of doubt: and this very circumstance brings out more clearly the grounds on which our belief in their inspiration rests. In proof of this, the Author begs leave to refer to his notes on Mark xvi. 9—20, and on John vii. 53; viii. 1—11.

[6] Cp. *Hooker*, V. xxii. 2.

for safe custody, near the Ark[7], in the Holy of Holies; and that they were ordered to be read at the Feast of Tabernacles as His Holy Word.

These commands of God were the first beginnings of a comprehensive Plan for the preservation of the Holy Scriptures, and for their publication to the world, and for the attestation of their divine origin and authority, by *external* evidence which all might see, and none could gainsay.

The ancient Hebrew Church read the Old Testament in the Synagogues, Sabbath after Sabbath, year after year, and century after century, in all parts of the world. It read the Old Testament as inspired by God.

And when the Son of God came down from heaven, He took part, as we have already seen[8], in this public reading of the Old Testament in the Hebrew Synagogues; He acknowledged the Old Testament, which was there read, to be what the ancient Hebrew Church believed and testified it to be,—the unerring Word of God.

2. This providential arrangement for the guardianship and authentication of God's Word, by means of public Reading, was maintained and enlarged, from the time of the writing of the first Books of the *Old Testament* until Christ's First Advent; and ever since that time it has been growing and expanding itself throughout

---

[7] See above, pp. 44—47. [8] See above, pp. 62—66.

the world by the planting and propagation of Christian Churches in distant lands; and it will continue to extend itself by the preaching of *the Gospel* as *a witness unto all Nations even unto the end* [9], when Christ will come again to judge the World.

This divinely-instituted plan of public Reading comprehends within its range the *New* Testament, as well as the Old; and places the *New* Testament on the same footing with the Old. This appears from the history of the publication and preservation of the New Testament.

One of the most remarkable portions of the New Testament in this particular respect, is that which we have been reading in the Church during the last week, namely, the First and Second Epistles of St. Paul to the Church of Thessalonica. These two Epistles were the *first* of all St. Paul's Epistles, and were among the first written of all the Books of the New Testament.

It is observable, that in the first of these two Epistles to the Thessalonians, St. Paul gives a solemn injunction, as follows: *I charge, or adjure you, by the Lord, that this Epistle be read unto all the holy brethren* [1]. *That* Epistle was to be *read openly* in the Church. And in another Epistle,—that to the Colossians,—St. Paul takes for granted that it also would be *read* in the Church. He thus speaks: *When this Epistle is read among you,*

---

[9] Matt. xxiv. 14.   [1] 1 Thess. v. 27.

cause that it be read also in the Church of the Laodiceans[2].

What St. Paul required to be done to his own Epistles, was done to all the Books of the New Testament. They were *received* and *read openly* and habitually on the Lord's Day, year after year and century after century, in Christian Churches, from primitive times[3].

And with what feelings were they received and read? Were they regarded as *common* writings? No: certainly not. They were received and read as the *Word of God*. They were reverently received as such; they were received and read as *Holy Scripture*[4]; they were read simultaneously with the Books of the *Old* Testament. They were read as *equally inspired* with the Books of *Moses* and the *Prophets*[5], which had been received by Christ Himself, as the Word of the Living God.

Thus the Holy Spirit, dwelling in the Church of God, bore witness to them, and testified that they are the Oracles of God[6].

[2] Col. iv. 16.   [3] See *Bingham*, Antiquities, XIV. ch. iii.

[4] It is remarkable that the word Γραφὴ, which simply means *writing*, is reserved and appropriated in the New Testament (where it occurs fifty times) to the *sacred* writings, i. e. to the *Holy Scriptures;* and marks the separation of the *Scriptures* from all "common books," indeed, from *all other writings* in the world; just as in English the words *Bible* (i. e. *book*) and *Scripture* (i. e. *writing*) have been consecrated for a like use.

[5] See *Bingham*, Antiquities, XIV. ch. iii.

[6] Cp. *Hooker*, V. xxii. 2: "The *reading* of the Word of God in open audience is the plainest evidence we have of the Church's assent and acknowledgment that it *is* His Word."

Some smaller portions of the New Testament were not received at once by all Churches.

3. Let us also consider this. The writers of the New Testament lay claim to Inspiration. Thus St. Paul says to the Corinthians, *I trow*[7] *that I have the Spirit of God*[8]. And, *We speak not in words which man's wisdom teacheth, but which the Holy Ghost teacheth*[9]. And he appeals to his miracles wrought among them in proof of his Inspiration. *Truly the signs of an Apostle were wrought among you in all patience, in signs, and wonders, and mighty deeds*[1].

The Epistles of St. Paul, in which these words occur, contain severe rebukes and censures of those to whom these Epistles were sent. He reproves them as *carnal*, as *babes in Christ*, and yet *puffed up*[2]. Those persons were proud of their intellectual and spiritual gifts; and the *reception* of those Epistles involved a condemnation of themselves. They would never have received those Epistles as inspired, unless they had been convinced, that the claims of the writer to Inspiration were true.

The reception of *all* the Books of the New Testament as of equally divine authority, is a proof of their Inspiration.

IV. But it may be asked,—

Are there not *some portions* of the *New Testament* which were *not* at first received universally as the inspired Word of God?

[7] δοκῶ.
[9] 1 Cor. ii. 13.
[2] 1 Cor. iii. 1—3; v. 2.
[8] 1 Cor. vii. 40.
[1] 2 Cor. xii. 12.

Inferences to be derived from partial non-reception, 91
and subsequent universal reception, of those portions.

Yes, certainly there are.

The *whole* primitive Church received the Four Gospels, and the Acts of the Apostles, the Thirteen Epistles which bear the name of St. Paul, and the First Epistle of St. Peter and of St. John. These Books were universally received *at once* by all Christendom, as soon as they were written.

But there are some *few minor parts* of the New Testament, concerning which *some particular* Churches at first suspended their judgment.

Such, for instance, was the Second Epistle of St. Peter. Some Churches waited for a time, and did not pronounce judgment upon that Epistle, till they were fully persuaded of its genuineness and inspiration. But, after careful examination, they received it; and eventually *all* Churches in Christendom *agreed* in receiving *all* the Books of the New Testament as the Word of God.

This very fact, that *some* of the Books of the New Testament were *not* received by all at first, is of great value. It proves the scrupulous care, with which those Books were *examined*, before they were received by the Church; and the fact also, that those Books, concerning which some Churches doubted at first, were eventually received by *all* Churches, proves that they were rightly received.

V. To this testimony of the Holy Ghost, dwelling in the Catholic Church, receiving the whole of the New Testament, we appeal in support of our belief that all of it is the Word of God.

Let us here obviate an objection.

Let it not be supposed, that we are of opinion with some in the Church of Rome[3], that the *Church* can *give authority* to *Scripture*. No; the authority of Scripture comes from God, and God alone. The light is not from the Candlestick, but from the Candles; it is not from the Church, but from the Scriptures, which are the Candles that Christ has lighted, and set in the Church. But the Church *testifies* to the divine authority of Scripture. John the Baptist was a *shining light*[4], and bore *witness* to Christ. That witness was true; for John was *full of the Holy Ghost*[5] Who spake by him. But John did not *give* any authority to Christ. So the Church bears testimony to Scripture, and we appeal to *that* testimony as true: we appeal to it as the testimony of Christ, and of the Holy Ghost.

And why? Because Christ has said, *that the gates of hell shall never prevail against His Church*[6], and *that He will be ever with her, and will send her the Holy Spirit to teach her all things, to guide her into all truth, and to abide with her for ever*[7].

If the New Testament, which the Universal Church receives and reads as the Word of God, is only the word of *man*; *if* the Church of God has *not* been led into truth in this vital matter; *if* the

---

[3] Whose assertions to this effect may be seen in the Author's volume on the Canon of Scripture, p. 15.
[4] λύχνος, *a lamp*. John v. 35.   [5] Luke i. 15.
[6] Matt. xvi. 18.   [7] John xiv. 16; xvi. 13.

whole Church of Christ has fallen into error in this fundamental article concerning the Inspiration of the New Testament, on which the fabric of her faith, and hope, and charity is built, then—we say it with all reverence—Christ's promise to His Church has failed. He has *not* sent the Holy Spirit to *teach her all things,* and *to lead her into all truth,* and *to abide with her for ever.*

But, God forbid, my brethren, that any one should imagine this!

Christ is the Truth. He is the everlasting *Yea* and *Amen*[8]. *Heaven and earth will pass away, but His words will not pass away*[9]. Therefore His promise of presence and guidance to His Church has *not* failed. He speaks to us by her, to whom He has sent His Spirit, and He assures us by her voice and practice that *all* the Books of the New Testament, which she reads as inspired, were given by the inspiration of God.

VI. Thanks be to God, the Church of England was endued with wisdom, at her Reformation in the sixteenth century, to build her belief, and her people's belief, in the Inspiration of Holy Scripture, on this good foundation.

1. *She* did *not* say,—what some *other* religious communities *did* say at that time[1],—that men's belief in the Inspiration of Scripture is to rest on their own inner illumination, or personal consciousness. She did *not* build her house on such

---

[8] Rev. iii. 14. Cp. 2 Cor. i. 20. [9] Luke xxi. 33.
[1] See above, pp. 23, 24.

a floating quicksand as that. No: she appealed to the public judgment and concurrent practice of the Church of Christ Universal. In her Sixth Article[2] she says, "In the name of the HOLY SCRIPTURE we do understand those Canonical Books of the OLD and NEW TESTAMENT, of whose authority was *never any doubt in the Church.*" And because she well knew that there are *some few portions* of the *New* Testament—such as the Second Epistle of St. Peter, as already stated— concerning which there *were some doubts* at first in *some* Churches, but which were afterwards universally received, without any doubt, by the *whole Catholic Church,* she wisely adds, at the close of the same Article: "All the Books of the *New* Testament, *as they are commonly received,* we do receive and account them canonical."

She also shows, *what* those Books are, by her Authorized Version of the Bible, and by her Calendar of Lessons of Holy Scripture, appointed to be read daily throughout the year.

2. We cannot be too thankful, that the Church of our beloved Country was mercifully preserved from building on an unsound foundation in this momentous matter. Three centuries have elapsed since that Article was published; and succeeding

---

[2] In the Thirty-nine Articles of the Church of England "as agreed upon by the Archbishops and Bishops of both Provinces and the whole Clergy, in the Convocation holden at London in the year 1562."

years bear witness to the wisdom with which it was framed.

We have seen, and now see, that *other* religious Communities,—particularly those foreign Protestant Churches,—which did *not* build on this foundation, but on the loose substructure of private opinion, or personal feeling, in this great question of Inspiration—have been, and are now, buffeted and bewildered by the winds and storms of Infidelity. They have separated Holy Scripture from the Church, which is the appointed Keeper and Guardian of Scripture; and therefore they have almost forfeited Scripture. There is scarcely any portion of the Bible, which has not now been gainsaid and rejected by some of their most eminent Teachers, relying with fond and overweening conceit on their own private imaginations, and dogmatizing rashly and recklessly on God's Holy Word, with arbitrary wilfulness, and disdainful contempt of Authority. They declaim loudly against the Papacy, but many a man among them sets up a private Popedom in his own person, and claims spiritual supremacy and infallibility for himself, and lords it over the faith of men. This self-confident dictation of crude, ill-digested opinions has engendered endless strife; this irrational abuse of reason, and injudicious perversion of private judgment, have brought discredit upon Reason, and have been disastrous to Faith.

3. Blessed be God, the Church of England has

not been led astray by this fanatical spirit. She has been enabled to discharge faithfully the duty of a Church in the public reading of Holy Writ. Blessed be God, she reads day by day, throughout the year, several chapters of Holy Scripture to the People in their mother tongue. Blessed also be God, she builds her belief in the Inspiration of Scripture on a sound foundation; she builds it on the testimony of Christ, speaking by His Church to the world.

4. This method of proof has been dictated by Christ Himself. *No man*, He says, *when he hath lighted a candle, putteth it in a secret place, neither under a bushel, but on a Candlestick, that they which come in may see the light.* And again, He said, *No man lighteth a candle and covereth it with a vessel, or putteth it under a bed; but setteth it on a Candlestick, that they which enter in may see the light.*

Christ is the *Light of the World*[3]. He lighted the candles of Holy Scripture, and He has put them into the Candlestick of His Church, which is appointed to guard and display the light of Holy Scripture kindled by Christ. Therefore Christ Himself, in the Book of Revelation, describes a *Church* under the figure of a *Candlestick*[4].

[3] John viii. 12; ix. 5.

[4] λυχνία—properly a *lamp-stand;* a term even more significant of this office of the Church, than the English word *candlestick;* for the lamp is fed with *oil*, which is an appropriate emblem of Holy Scripture, bestowed by the Holy Spirit, the Giver of Divine unction and grace, illuminating the world. See Rev. i. 11—13.

in which the Candles of Scripture are lighted and set by Christ.

Observe those seven-branched Candlesticks standing before the Altar of this Church. They are now dark. And why? Because they have no candles in them. Such is a Church without Scripture. It is dark; a Candlestick without light. But put the Candles of Scripture into the Candlestick of the Church, and all may see the light.

Again, if you light the candles, but put them into a vault or crypt [5], or if you strew them on the ground, the candles are of little use; they soon go out. So, if you bury the Bible in the crypt and vault of a dead language, it is of little use. If you hide it from the people, it is of little use. Or if you cover it with the bushel of secular business, or put it beneath the bed of carnal indulgence, it is of little use.

Or if, on the other hand, you scatter Bibles about at random, and do not put them into the Candlestick of the Church, they will be puffed and blown about with every wind of doctrine, and will flare and smoke, and soon go out.

We must have the Candles, and we must have the Candlestick; and the Candles must be put into the Candlestick, and they will give light to all.

Christ has lighted the Candles of Holy Scripture, and He has set them in the Candlestick of His Church. Let us not separate the Candles from the Candlestick, lest we derive no profit

[5] κρύπτην, the true reading in the text, Luke xi. 33.

98 *They who separate the Bible from the Church, are in peril of losing both the Bible and the Church.*

from either. Let us not sever the Bible from the Church, lest we lose both.

5. Look up to heaven. Behold Christ. *He is the true Light that lighteth every man that cometh into the world* [6]. He enlightened Moses, He enlightened the Prophets *before* His Incarnation; He enlightened the Apostles and Evangelists *after* His Incarnation. He sent the Holy Ghost to *teach them all things, and to guide them into all truth, and to bring to their remembrance whatsoever He had said unto them,* and to diffuse the light of the Holy Scriptures, *which are able to make us wise unto salvation through faith in Him* [7].

Christ, the Everlasting WORD, is the Author and Giver of the written Word [8].

6. Further, Christ is the Truth. He is *the Way, the Truth, and the Life* [9]. He *is the faithful and true Witness* [1]. He gave the Scriptures, and also bears testimony to their Inspiration. When He came down from Heaven and took our flesh, He acknowledged all the Books of the Old Testament to be given by Inspiration of God. And after His ascension into heaven, He established His Church, and sent the Holy Spirit to

---

[6] John i. 9.   [7] 2 Tim. iii. 15.

[8] *S. Augustine* de Consens. Evangel. lib. i. cap. ult. well says, " Qui Prophetas *ante* Suam descensionem misit, Ipse et Apostolos post Suam ascensionem misit ... quicquid Ille de Suis factis et dictis nos legere voluit, hoc scribendum illis tanquam Suis manibus imperavit." See also the passages quoted in the Preface to these Lectures.

[9] John xiv. 6.   [1] Rev. iii. 14.

They who separate the Bible from the Church, are in peril of losing both the Bible and the Church.

teach *her all things,* and to *guide her into all truth,* and to be for ever with her. The Holy Ghost speaks in her, and by her, and declares by her voice and practice, that the Scriptures of the Old and New Testaments are the Word of the Living God.

VII. Lastly, Christ gives the Holy Spirit to all those who seek for Him aright. He punishes ungodly men with spiritual blindness, so that they cannot see the light shining in Holy Scripture. He chastises those who lead unholy lives, who would quench the light of Scripture, if they could, for it speaks to them of a Judgment to come. He allows them to close their eyes, and leaves them to themselves. Infidelity is the punishment which evil men inflict on themselves by their sins. *Every one that doeth evil hateth the light, neither cometh to the light, lest his deeds should be reproved*[2]. Nor is it only carnal indulgence, or worldliness, which produce spiritual blindness. Spiritual blindness often co-exists with great mental endowments. It is engendered by intellectual pride. God hides Himself *from the wise and prudent, but revealeth Himself unto babes*[3]. *He resisteth the proud, but giveth grace unto the humble*[4]. They who carp and cavil at Scripture, they who deny the truth and inspiration of Scripture, do despite to the Holy Spirit of God, who testifies to the divine authority of

[2] John iii. 20.   [3] Luke x. 21.
[4] James iv. 6. 1 Pet. v. 5.

Scripture. They *grieve the Holy Ghost.* They provoke Him to leave them to themselves. And how can they see without Him who is the Light? Their cavils against Scripture are precisely what might be expected. They are proofs of the blindness which is their chastisement for sinning against God the Holy Ghost.

The angels of Christ's little ones see the face of God[5]. We must *become as little children,* if we would behold Him, and see the *wondrous things of His Law*[6]. In order that the mind may be clear, the heart must be clean. We must seek for the truth, not by proud disputations, but by loving thoughts and words and deeds, by lowly reverence on our knees. We must seek it by holiness of life. *If any man willeth to do God's will, he shall also know of the doctrine*[7]. If any man *love God, the same is known of God*[8], and is loved of God, and God reveals Himself to him. *Mysteries are revealed unto the meek*[9]. *Them that are meek shall He guide in judgment; and such as are gentle, them shall He learn His way* [1].

Is this temper yours? Are these dispositions yours? Then, God knows, you will be enchanted and enraptured with the beauty and loveliness of Holy Scripture; you will be transported with holy ecstacy in hearing and reading it. It will sound in your ears like heavenly music, chanted by the quires of the Seraphim. By the aid of the Holy

[5] Matt. xviii. 10. [6] Ps. cxix. 18. [7] John vii. 17.
[8] 1 Cor. viii. 3. [9] Ecclus. iii. 19. [1] Ps. xxv. 8.

External evidence confirmed by internal. 101

Spirit *shed abroad in your hearts,* in answer to your prayers, you will see the work of the Spirit in the Bible. You will say, *Lord, how I love Thy Law, all the day long is my study in it. I rejoice at Thy Word as one that findeth great spoil*[2]. *Thy testimonies are my delight and my counsellors*[3]. *More to be desired are they than gold, yea, than much fine gold, sweeter also than honey, and the honeycomb*[4]. You will never be weary of admiring the harmonious symmetry of all the parts of the Bible, the unsullied holiness of its precepts, the exact fulfilment of its prophecies, the tender graciousness of its promises, the marvellous glory of its revelations, displaying Christ the *Sun of Righteousness,* illumining our dark nature with the brilliant splendour of His light, and dwelling therein with the Shechinah of His Presence, and pouring upon it the riches of His grace, and preparing it for the everlasting fruition of heavenly bliss. You will never be tired of meditating on the wonderful adaptation of the Scriptures to our nature and our needs, to our cares and our sorrows, to our fears and our hopes, to our temptations and our trials; you will never be satiated in contemplating the manifold blessings which have been produced by the Holy Scriptures in human hearts, and in human households, and in cities, kingdoms, and nations, wherever the Scriptures have been duly received, loved, and obeyed.

[2] Ps. cxix. 162. [3] Ps. cxix. 24. 97.
[4] Ps. xix. 10.

Thus you will be confirmed, settled, and immoveably established in your belief, which Christ, speaking in His Church, solemnly testifies to be true, that *all Scripture is given by Inspiration of God*[5]. And you may humbly believe and devoutly hope, that, if you have profited aright by its revelations upon earth, it will be your employment and joy, in a future, eternal state of existence, to have a fuller insight into those Mysteries, of which the Scriptures speak, and which *Angels desire to look into*[6]; and to have an everlasting vision in heaven, of the manifold wisdom of God.

[5] 2 Tim. iii. 16.   [6] 1 Pet. i. 12.

LECTURE V.

2 Timothy iii. 16, 17.

All Scripture is given by inspiration of God, and is profitable for doctrine, for reproof, for correction, for instruction in righteousness; that the man of God may be perfect, throughly furnished unto all good works.

I. *Be ready always to give an answer to every man that asketh you a reason of the hope that is in you.* This is the precept of St. Peter[1]. The hope that is in us, is grounded on a belief that the Bible is the Word of God; and the Apostle may therefore be understood to require us to be ready always to render to others an account of the reasons which constrain us, and ought to persuade them, to receive the Bible as God's Holy Word.

1. This being the case, we have in a previous lecture[2] declared ourselves unable to agree with those, who rest their belief in the Inspiration of the Bible on their own personal assurance of its Inspiration. Such an assurance, however satisfactory to *themselves,* can have no influence with

[1] 1 Pet. iii. 15.   [2] See above, pp. 20—24.

other men; it will never bring an unbeliever to acknowledge the Bible to be from God.

2. Besides, the history of the last three centuries, and especially of our own age, has displayed the disastrous consequences of such a method of dealing with this great question of Inspiration.

The appeal to private feelings and assurances was first employed in *defence* of the Bible; but it has now been turned *against* it; and they who rely on private feelings and personal assurances, as their ground for *believing* the Bible, cannot make any effectual reply to those who appeal to their own private feelings and personal assurances as their reason for *rejecting* it.

The dogmas of Private Judgment have produced the doubts of Infidelity. The advantages which have been given to Scepticism by that appeal to personal feelings and private opinions, and the baneful fruits which it is now bringing forth in our own land, warn us most solemnly to consider well our first principles.

3. We need something much more sound, solid, and stable, than our own consciousness, to refute the assaults of Unbelief, and to sustain our own faith and that of others in the divine Inspiration of the Bible; and also, if God so will, to bring the Sceptic and Unbeliever to acknowledge that *all Scripture is given by Inspiration of God.*

4. It has been my endeavour to do something, with God's help, in this great work *of building up*

our old waste places, and raising up the foundations of many generations[3] and *repairing the breach* that has been made by some, who ought themselves to be builders; and with this aim and purpose, the Discourses have been delivered on this subject which have been lately addressed to you in this place.

Reasonable men require sound reasons for what they do; and their assent to any proposition is proportioned to the reasons given in support of it; and the influence, which any proposition exercises on their conduct, is also proportioned to the conviction produced by those reasons in their minds.

II. What, then, are our *reasons* for belief in the Inspiration of Holy Scripture?

1. Our answer to this question, as you may remember, was: We have the authority of GOD Himself, declared to us in the uniform consent and practice of His own People, acknowledging the Old Testament to be His Word. We have that acknowledgment authorized and confirmed by the SON of GOD, when He came down from heaven and dwelt among us. And for our belief in the Inspiration of the New Testament as well as of the Old, we have the testimony of the Son of God, speaking by the voice of GOD the HOLY GHOST in the Church Universal, to which He has promised His presence and His guidance, even to the end.

[3] Isa. lviii. 12.

106 *The previous proof of the Inspiration of the Bible is confirmed by the evidence of God's care of the Bible.*

2. The value of this testimony to the Inspiration of Holy Scripture is its comprehensiveness and universality. *Other* arguments apply with greater or less force to *portions* of Holy Writ. But *this* testimony extends to the *whole Bible.* It covers the whole with a divine panoply. It authenticates the whole as the Inspired Word of God; it proves, that *all Scripture—every part of Scripture—is given by Inspiration of God.*

III. To this point in the argument we had arrived in the last discourse.

Let us now proceed to observe, that the strength of this general testimony of God the Son, and of God the Holy Ghost, to the Inspiration of Holy Scripture, is corroborated by other subsequent considerations, which accrue with cumulative force, and settle and stablish us more firmly in the belief, that the Scriptures are the Word of God.

What, then, are these considerations? This will be the subject of our present inquiry.

1. First, then, we are confirmed in our belief of the Inspiration of the Bible by observing the evidences of a *providential design* carried on during many ages in succession, for *protecting* the Bible, and for *assuring* us that *Holy Scripture is God's Word.*

If the Bible were *not* His Word, it would be nothing else than a *forgery* put forth in His name. For, it professes to deliver a message from God, and to give revelations of His nature and attributes, and to unfold the hidden mysteries of the spiritual world.

If, therefore, the Bible is *not* from God, it is a counterfeit coin, bearing His impress: it is a profane outrage against Him, and a fraudulent imposture upon mankind. Consequently it would be viewed with indignation by Him Who is a God of justice and truth.

But look back upon the past. Ever since the Bible was written, Almighty God has continued to *protect* it. He has never ceased to acknowledge it as His own. When the first books of the Bible —namely, the books of Moses—were written, He received them under His divine guardianship in the Holy of Holies[4]. In critical times, He has ever interfered to save it. When the Old Testament was in peril of being lost, through the corruption and idolatry of Princes, Priests and People, He brought forth the original volume of the Law from its sacred retreat in the days of good King Josiah, who in his own name, and in that of his people, proclaimed it to be the Word of God[5].

The subsequent *dispersion* of the *Jews* for their sins was made ministerial, as we have seen[6], to the preservation and dissemination of God's Holy Word in almost all countries, where Synagogues were erected by the Jews, in which

---

[4] See above, pp. 44, 45.   [5] See above, p. 45.
[6] See above, pp. 38—40. 53, 54.

the Old Testament was publicly read every Sabbath day.

Afterwards, in an evil time, Antiochus Epiphanes the King of Syria arose, and set up the abomination of desolation in the Temple of God at Jerusalem; and endeavoured to compel the Jews to worship the gods of the Heathen; and sent forth his own soldiers to destroy the copies of the Old Testament, who *rent in pieces the Books of the Law which they found, and burnt them with fire; and whosoever was found* with any such Book *was put to death* by the King's command[7].

In that critical juncture Almighty God interposed to rescue His own Word, and the persecuting King was suddenly cut off by a miserable death[8].

About a century and a half passed away, and the Son of God came down from heaven. At that time the Word of God was publicly read by the Jews in the Synagogues of Palestine, and in almost every city of the civilized world. But its sense was overlaid and obscured by human traditions. The Son of God acknowledged the Old Testament in the hands of the Jews. He owned it to be God's Word. He showed His zeal for it by sternly rebuking the Pharisees for making it of *none effect by their tradition*[9]. But He never rebuked them for receiving it as God's Word.

---

[7] 1 Mac. i. 54, 55—57.
[8] 1 Mac. vi. 12, 13. 16. 2 Mac. ix. 11—18. 28.
[9] Matt. xv. 3. 6.

No: on the contrary, He joined with them in the service of their Synagogues, and in reading and expounding the Old Testament as God's Word[1]. And His Apostles, and His Church after them, being taught by the Holy Ghost, sent by the Son of God, received the Old Testament as inspired by God; and commanded all men to receive it as such.

At the beginning of the fourth century after Christ, a fierce persecution arose against His Church. The Emperor of the Roman World, Diocletian, endeavoured to destroy the Bible. He ordered diligent search to be made in all parts of the Empire for copies of the New Testament[2], and commanded them to be burnt. But God again interfered to save it. The sacred Bush *was burning, but it was not consumed,* and God's voice came forth from the midst of it[3]. In a few years afterwards, He raised up another Sovereign of the Roman World, Constantine, the first Emperor who embraced Christianity; and by his royal command copies of the Holy Scriptures were multiplied, and Churches were built, in which those Scriptures were read, as the Inspired Word of God.

A thousand years passed away. Then was an evil time for Holy Scripture. The Bible was not dead; but it was buried. It was entombed in the

---

[1] See above, pp. 62—69.   [2] *Euseb.* H. E. viii. 2.
[3] Exod. iii. 2. 4.

sepulchre of a dead language. Not to speak of other lands, but only of our own, not a single copy of the Bible existed at that time in England in our tongue. But then arose John Wickliffe. Five hundred years ago, he translated the Bible into English[4]. In that age copies of the Bible could only be had in *manuscript;* and four and twenty years after his death it was decreed[5] by some in high place among us, that "no one should hereafter translate any text into English, and that no book of this kind should be read that was composed by John Wickliffe."

There was then a *famine of hearing God's Word*[6] in England.

But in fifty years' time, the art of Printing was invented, and William Caxton set up his press at Westminster[7]. And about the year 1526 William Tyndal made and published in London his Translation of the Bible—the *first* Translation that ever was *printed* in this land. The Author of this Translation, and his coadjutor John Frith, died nobly as Martyrs for the Faith; and the light which they kindled has never been put out. Two centuries and a half *after* the *first* Translation of the Bible into English by Wickliffe, and about two centuries and a half ago,—that is, in the year of our Lord 1611.—our own "Authorized Version"

---

[4] See *Lewis*, History of English Translations of the Bible, pp. 18—27. Lond. 1739.

[5] By Archbishop Arundel, in a Constitution at Oxford, 1408.

[6] Amos viii. 11.   [7] A.D. 1474.

was published. That noble Translation was made by a goodly company of pious and learned men, at the head of whom stood a Dean of Westminster[8]; and by God's blessing on their labours, and on those of others in this and other lands, especially our religious Societies, the Holy Scriptures are now diffused everywhere. *Their sound is gone out into all lands, and their words into the ends of the world*[9]. *This is the Lord's doing, and it is marvellous in our eyes*[1].

Surely these events, extending over a range of more than three thousand years, afford practical attestation from God Himself, that the Bible is His Word. Surely they may inspire us with the cheering assurance, that, however Satan may assail it, God will protect it unto the end.

2. Another evidence of the Inspiration of Holy Scripture is seen in *the fulfilment of the Prophecies*, which are contained therein. God, and God alone, can foresee the future. He challenges false gods by saying, " *Show us what shall happen, declare us things for to come*[2]."

Let this test be applied to the Books of the Old Testament.

Can any *other* writings in the world be named, composed at such different times, in such different places, and by the instrumentality of such dif-

---

[8] Dean—afterwards Bishop—Andrewes. See *Lewis's* History of the Translations of the Bible, p. 308.

[9] Ps. xix. 4.   [1] Ps. cxviii. 23.

[2] Isa. xli. 22.

ferent persons, as the Books of the Old Testament; and delivering such a long series of Prophecies, as those, for instance, which concern the Messiah, and begin with the Book of Genesis, and end with that of Malachi; can any other writings be named, containing Prophecies so minute, so various, and *seemingly* so contradictory—as, for example, those which pre-announce a Messiah, *suffering* the most shameful and agonizing death, and yet *triumphing* as a mighty Conqueror, and *reigning* as a glorious King—and all punctually fulfilled, fulfilled by the agency of that very people—the Jews—who heard those prophecies *every Sabbath day* in their Synagogues; and yet, as St. Paul says, *fulfilled them in condemning Him* of whom those Prophecies speak?

Here, then, is another proof that the Books of the Old Testament are animated by the breath of God.

3. Consider also the wonderful *symmetry of the various parts of the Bible.*

Its subject-matter reaches from the Creation to the End of time. Its Books were written by different persons in distant ages and countries. And yet how marvellously do they harmonize together! They are like Christ's *vesture, woven without seam* [3]. They are like the wings of the Cherubim, as described by Ezekiel, intertwined and interlaced together [4]. The Jewish Doctors said that the

---

[3] John xix. 23.   [4] Ezek. i. 9. 11, 12.

The harmony of the various parts of the Bible confirms the proof of its Inspiration.

words of the Pentateuch make *one word;* and there is a spiritual truth in the saying. The Books of the Bible are all fitted together. The Law prepares the way for the Prophets, and the Prophets proclaim the Sanctity of the Law. The New Testament lies hid in the Old Testament, and the Old Testament is opened in the New. All the Books of the Bible are joined together, and form *one Book.*

No human design could have produced such a result as this. It is the work of Him who sees all things at a glance *to the end from the beginning*[5], and with Whom *one day is as a thousand years, and a thousand years as one day*[6].

Here is another evidence that the Bible is from God.

4. Let us also reflect *what kind of persons* they were, who were *employed* to *write* the Bible.

The Bible, particularly the New Testament, professes to unfold things *hidden from the foundation of the world*[7]. The Gospels claim to be records of the sayings of the Son of God, revealing the secret Mysteries of His heavenly Kingdom. And *who* were the persons *chosen* to write these marvels? Their enemies justly said that they were *unlearned and ignorant men*[8]. True: such they were in *themselves,* Publicans and Fishermen of Galilee. Yet these *unlearned and ignorant* men

---

[5] Isa. xlvi. 10.
[7] Matt. xiii. 35.
[6] 2 Pet. iii. 8.
[8] Acts iv. 13.

have become the Teachers of the World. They are the Historians of the greatest deeds that ever were done; they are the Chroniclers of the wisest sayings that were ever spoken, and they are the utterers of the most heavenly Sermons that were ever preached. And the World has received their words,—has received them as divine. The Gospels are read everywhere. God has evangelized the learned and wise by means of the simple and foolish; and not the simple and foolish by means of the learned and wise. As S. Augustine says, "He caught the Orator by the Fisherman; and not the Fisherman by the Orator [9]."

The greatest sages of this world—the Bacons and Newtons, the Keplers and Pascals—have deemed it their highest privilege to sit down as little children at the feet of the holy Evangelists.

How could this be done?

Certainly not by the writers themselves. *Of themselves they could do nothing. Their sufficiency was of God* [1]. But according to His promise, Christ sent the Holy Ghost, *to lead them into all truth, and to bring all things to their remembrance, whatsoever He had said to them.*

He *chose weak instruments* for this *mighty work* of evangelizing the world, in order that by the *weakness of the instruments chosen,* and by the

---

[9] Piscatorem de Oratore non lucratus est Christus, sed Oratorem de Piscatore. *S. Augustine,* de Utilitate Jejunii ix., and Serm. xliii. and lxxxvii., and in Ps. cxlix.

[1] 2 Cor. iii. 5.

The beneficial effects produced by the Bible 115
prove it to be of God.

greatness of the work done through their instrumentality, it might be evident to all, that the work was not of them, but of God. The treasure of heavenly truth was committed to earthen vessels, in order that the *excellency of the power of the Gospel* might be seen *to be of God, and not of men* ².

5. Let us reflect also on the beneficent *effects produced* by *the Bible* on the world.

Here is another proof that the Scriptures are from God. The Bible speaks in God's name, and professes to be God's Word. And *if* it is not in fact what in name it professes to be, then it has a lie in every page, and it is not from God, but from the Evil One. *Every plant, which My Heavenly Father hath not planted, shall be rooted up,* says Christ³. And, *A Tree is known by its fruits*⁴.

What, then, have been the *fruits* of the Bible?

Do they not show that the tree is a good tree, that it is a tree of life, and *that its leaves are for the healing of the Nations* ⁵ ?

This is the fact on which St. Paul insists, when he says that *All Scripture,* or rather *every Scripture*⁶, *being divinely inspired,* or *inbreathed by God, is also* ⁷ *profitable for doctrine, for reproof, for correction, for instruction in righteousness, that the man of God may be perfect, throughly furnished*

² 2 Cor. iv. 7. ³ Matt. xv. 13.
⁴ Matt. vii. 16; xii. 33. Luke vi. 43. ⁵ Rev. xxii. 2.
⁶ πᾶσα γραφή i. e. Every portion of the Holy Book is inspired, and forms a living portion of a living organic whole.
⁷ καί; this is probably the true reading of the text.

I 2

unto every good work. What is the condition of men without it? and what is their condition, wherever they receive and obey it? The Bible, and the Bible alone, makes subjects loyal to their Sovereigns, because it teaches them that, in obeying their Sovereign, they are obeying God, and will be rewarded hereafter by Him [8]. The Bible, and the Bible alone, makes Sovereigns rule rightly, because it reminds them that they must render a strict account of their rule to the King of kings. The Bible makes Judges and Magistrates judge just judgment, because it tells them, that they must one day stand before the Judgment-seat of Christ. The Bible makes Masters kind to their Servants, because it declares to all Masters, that they have *a Master in heaven* [9]. The Bible makes Servants faithful to their Masters, because it assures all Servants that they are Christ's *freemen*, and will receive a reward for dutiful service, at the Great Day [1]. The Bible persuades busy men to forego their business, and makes tender women forget their tenderness, and visit Prisons and Hospitals, and minister at the bedside of the sick, and watch over the dying; because they know, that what they do to *the least of Christ's brethren* on earth, they do *it unto Him*, and that He will requite them for it at the Great Day [2]. The Bible, and the Bible alone, unlocks the

---

[8] Rom. xiii. 1—3.   [9] Eph. vi. 9. Col. iv. 1.
[1] Eph. vi. 5. Col. iii. 22. Titus ii. 9. 1 Pet. ii. 18. 22.
[2] Matt. xxv. 40.

The beneficial effects produced by the Bible, in nations and families, prove it to be of God.

fetters of the slave, and makes all men *brethren in Christ*³. The Bible sends forth the Missionary to heathen lands, to loose the chains of the soul. The Bible, and the Bible alone, operates on the mainspring of human actions—*the heart*. The Bible makes men honest and just, kind and charitable in their *thoughts* and *speeches,* as well as in their *acts,* because it teaches them, that *all things are naked and open to the eyes of Him with Whom they have to do* ⁴, and that He will bring *to light the hidden things of darkness, and make manifest the counsels of the hearts* ⁵. The Bible makes Husbands and Wives faithful and loving to each other, because it teaches, that Marriage was instituted by God in Paradise, and that it represents the spiritual union and wedlock between Christ and His Church, and that whoever dishonours Marriage desecrates a great Mystery ⁶. The Bible makes young men and young women live pure, chaste, and holy lives, because it teaches them that *their bodies are temples of the Holy Ghost,* and that whosoever *defiles the Temple of God, him will God destroy* ⁷, and that *their bodies are members of Christ,* and are to be held *in honour* as such ⁸; and that their bodies will be raised again from the grave, and that they must then give an account of the *things done in the body* ⁹, and that, if they

³ Philem. 16.
⁵ 1 Cor. iv. 5.
⁷ 1 Cor. iii. 16, 17; vi. 19.
⁹ Rom ii. 6; xiv. 12. 2 Cor. v. 10.

⁴ Heb. iv. 13.
⁶ Eph. v. 22—32.
⁸ 1 Cor. vi. 15. 1 Thess. iv. 4.

have presented their bodies a *living sacrifice* to God upon earth[1], in holiness and pureness of living, their bodies will rise from the grave, and live hereafter in heaven, in everlasting health and angelic beauty, and *be made like unto Christ's glorious body, according to the mighty working whereby He is able to subdue all things unto Himself*[2].

What shall we say more? The Bible is the fountain of all true Patriotism and Loyalty in States; it is the source of all true wisdom, sound policy and equity in Senates, Council-chambers, and Courts of Justice; it is the spring of all true discipline and obedience, and of all valour and chivalry in Armies and Fleets, on the battle-field, and on the wide sea. It is the origin of all probity and integrity in Commerce and in Trade, in Marts and in Shops, in Banking-houses and Exchanges; in the public resorts of men, and in the secret silence of the heart. It is the pure unsullied fountain of all love and peace, happiness, quietness, and joy, in families and households. Wherever it is duly obeyed, it makes the *desert* of the World *to rejoice and blossom as the rose*[3].

These are the fruits of the Bible. Surely we may conclude from them, that the Tree which bears them has been planted by the hand of God, and is watered by the dews and showers of His Spirit, and is warmed by the sunshine of His

---

[1] Rom. xii. 1. [2] Phil. iii. 21.
[3] Isa. xxxv. 1.

grace;—that it is God's Tree, and will flourish for evermore.

IV. Finally, let us look around. The place in which we now are, is full of instruction. In this ancient Minster, Kings and Queens are crowned: and at their Coronation, that Sacred Volume, the HOLY BIBLE, is taken from that Altar; and that Blessed Book is placed in the Monarch's hands, with these solemn words, uttered by the public Voice of the English Church and Nation, at that august ceremonial [4]:—

"Our Gracious Sovereign! we present you with this Book, the most valuable thing that this world affords. Here is Wisdom; this is the Royal Law; these are the lively Oracles of God. Blessed is he that readeth, and they that keep the Words of this Book; that keep and do the things contained in it. For these are the words of eternal Life, able to make you wise and happy in this world, nay, wise unto salvation; and so, happy for evermore, through faith which is in Christ Jesus; to whom be glory for ever. Amen."

Again look around. We are assembled here to-day on the eve of a funeral—the funeral of the venerated Mother of our beloved Queen. Meditations on royal deaths, and on royal funerals, find a proper place here. For here Kings and

---

[4] See the "Form and Order of Coronation of the Kings and Queens of Great Britain and Ireland, in the Abbey Church of St. Peter, Westminster."

Queens rest in their graves. Here Princes and Nobles sleep in the dust. Here lie Statesmen and Orators, Legislators and Judges, Philosophers, Poets, and Historians, Captains and Conquerors.

Now consider this. We have indeed disclaimed the notion of some, that the feelings of man afford an adequate evidence of the truth of God. But heaven forbid that we should entertain a doubt that the Word of God finds a genuine response in the heart of man. What then shall we here say?

At their last hour, when the shadows of death were falling upon them, when the heart was beating feebly and faintly, and the hand could hardly prop the drooping head, when the eyes were beginning to be bedimmed with the cloud and mist of mortality, where, then, was their stay and support? At that awful hour, did the Sovereign find any solid comfort in meditating on the vast extent of his dominions, or on the long duration of his reign? No. Did the Princes and Nobles, who here lie buried, derive any real consolation from the splendour of their stately mansions, or the beauty of their wide demesnes, or from their patrician badges and titles, and the long line of their ancestral dignities? No: at that solemn hour, all these were vanishing like a dream. Did the Statesman obtain any comfortable assurance from his political sagacity, or the Orator from his brilliant eloquence? No: these things were like fading flowers. Did the Legislator or the Judge find any assistance in their Codes and Law Books? No: they themselves were summoned to Judgment. Could the Philosopher solace himself with musing on his Problems and Theories, or the Poet with the remembrance of his songs? No: these *were like a tale that is told*[5]. Could the Historian procure peace for his soul from his records of past ages? No: he himself was passing away. Could the seafaring Captain obtain a spiritual calm from his long voyages to distant climes? No: he must now take another voyage to an unexplored region, where no earthly chart or compass would guide him. He must now set sail for Eternity. Did the General or Admiral,—the heroes of many battles,—gather hope and joy for themselves from their laurels gained in the conflicts of war? No: they must prepare now for a sharper struggle with Spiritual Powers, against which the Artillery of this world would be of no avail. But, had they, then, *no* comfort in that hour of Death? Miserable, miserable indeed, if such was then the case! Had they no comfort? And if they had, where was it? It was in the Bible. If they had believed its doctrines, and had obeyed its precepts, and if they had trusted in its promises, if they had lived and fed on it as living bread from heaven, then there was hope in their end. Then there was peace in their death, through the might and mercy of Him who died for them, and was buried, and overcame, and rose again, and opened the kingdom

[5] Ps. xc. 9.

of heaven to all believers. Then, though *they walked through the valley and shadow of death, they feared no evil, for He was with them* [6]. Then they fell asleep in peace, and in hope to awake with joy. Then *Death* to them was *Birth,—Birth* to *endless life.* Then they felt in their inmost hearts, that belief in the inspiration of the Bible —a belief based on the soundest reason—*is* able to speak comfort to the soul. Then they realized its power. Then it proved its virtue. Then they knew that *whatsoever had been written aforetime had been written for their learning, that they through patience and comfort of the Scriptures might have hope*[7]. Then they found, by personal experience, that a few verses of the Bible, heard with the ear of faith, are of more worth than crowns and coronets; that they are of more value than all the wealth and grandeur, all the mansions and estates, all the eloquence and wisdom, all the genius and science, all the triumphs and trophies, of this world. Then they drank a refreshing stream of heavenly peace and joy from such blessed words as these, *I am the Resurrection and the Life,* saith the Lord: *he that believeth in Me, though he were dead, yet shall he live: and he that liveth and believeth in Me shall never die*[8]. *Verily, verily, I say unto you, He that heareth My word, and believeth on Him that sent Me, hath everlasting life, and shall not come into condemnation, but is passed from*

---

[6] Ps. xxiii. 4.   [7] Rom. xv. 4.   [8] John xi. 25, 26.

The Day of Judgment will prove the truth of the Bible.

death unto life⁹. Then they were able to say, *O Death, where is thy sting? O Grave, where is thy Victory? Thanks be to God who giveth us the Victory through our Lord Jesus Christ* ¹. Then there was divine music for them in those heavenly words, *I heard a voice from heaven, saying unto me, Write, Blessed are the dead which die in the Lord: Even so, saith the Spirit, for they rest from their labours* ².

Brethren, may this support be ours, in our last hour! It *will be* ours, be sure, if we live and die in the belief, that *all Scripture is given by inspiration of God.* And hereafter, at the great and dreadful Day, when the *Elements shall melt with fervent heat*³, and when the Volume of this visible Creation will no more be legible; when all the fair characters now written in earth and sky upon the pages of the book of Nature, will be effaced and obliterated, and the heavens themselves *will depart as a scroll*⁴,—then the WORD of GOD will remain unchanged; its letters are indelible, they will *endure for ever* ⁵. *Heaven and earth shall pass away,* says Christ, *but My Words shall not pass away* ⁶. Blessed, therefore, is he that heareth and keepeth *the sayings of that Book* ⁷, blessed indeed is he—blessed for evermore!

⁹ John v. 24.
² Rev. xiv. 13.
⁴ Isa. xxxiv. 4. Rev. vi. 14.
⁶ Matt. xxiv. 35.
¹ 1 Cor. xv. 55.
³ 2 Pet. iii. 10.
⁵ 1 Pet. i. 25.
⁷ Rev. i. 3; xxii. 7.

www.ingramcontent.com/pod-product-compliance
Lightning Source LLC
Chambersburg PA
CBHW022134160426
43197CB00009B/1278